CHOPSTICKS RECIPES

MORE DIM SUM

D1564823

美點佳餚 8
南北點心
歐陽玅詩編著

Published and Distributed by
Chopsticks Publications Ltd.
P.O. Box 73515, Kowloon Central Post Office, Kowloon, Hong Kong.
108 Boundary St., G/F., Kowloon, Hong Kong.
144A Boundary St., 3/F., Kowloon, Hong Kong.
Tel.: 3-368433   3-390454

© Cecilia J. AU-YEUNG

All rights reserved
New revised edition
2nd print March 1989

ISBN 962 7018 68 6
Photography by Wilson Au-yeung
                    Au-yeung Chiu Mei
Edited by Caroline Au-yeung

UK Sole Distributor:
Gazelle Book Services
Falcon House Queen Square
Lancaster LA1 1RN
England

US Sole Distributor:
Seven Hills Distributors
49 Central Avenue
Cincinnati
Ohio 45202
USA

出版者及總批發
嘉饌出版有限公司

香港　九龍中央郵箱73515號
香港　九龍界限街108號地下
香港　九龍界限街144A號四樓
電話：3-368433, 3-390454
本書版權所有不得翻印或轉載

FOREWORD

Due to the popularity of my previous cookbook on Dim Sum, namely, 'Chopsticks Recipes' Book 2, published in June, 1976, I have now published Book 8 to introduce more Dim Sums. During the past few years, I have received a lot of letters from my readers, demanding for more Dim Sum recipes. Here, I would like to thank you for your overwhelming support.

In this book, I have included some dishes which are very simple and easy to make. My purpose is to publish a cookbook which is not merely for the professionals, but also for anyone who wants to know more about Dim Sum cooking. Other recipes in this cookbook are especially for people who live away from Hong Kong. Those who appreciate some rarer Dim Sum dishes often find difficulties in ordering them in most Chinese restaurants abroad. To solve the problem, what is simpler than to make the dish yourself? Besides Cantonese Dim Sum, I have also put in Dim Sum recipes from Northern China to increase the variety.

For the readers who have purchased Book 2, this book will broaden your knowledge and skill in Dim Sum cooking. I must add that Book 2 and Book 8 together include nearly all Chinese snacks.

I have done my utmost to make this cookbook worth your while to keep, and I am sure that you will relish the result of each recipe you try out.

Cecilia J. Au-yeung

CONTENTS

目　錄

义燒焗餐飽
Baked Cha Shiu Bread

材料

酵種—依士1茶匙
　　　糖½茶匙
　　　溫水¼杯
　　　筋粉3湯匙

麵糰—筋粉10安（280克）
　　　糖2安（56克）
　　　鷄蛋1隻
　　　淡奶1湯匙
　　　溫水⅓杯
　　　溶牛油2湯匙

餡料—叉燒8安（224克）
　　　水½杯
　　　蠔油2茶匙
　　　糖1茶匙
　　　胡椒粉少許
　　　蔴油½茶匙
　　　生粉水2湯匙
　　　葱粒2湯匙

製法：

酵種—
* 依士與糖洒在溫水中，以毛巾蓋住發10分鐘，篩入筋粉拌勻成粉漿，再發10分鐘。

麵糰—
* 筋粉篩在桌上開穴。放入糖、蛋、淡奶、酵種及溫水拌勻，慢慢將四週之粉撥入和勻。倒入溶牛油搓成軟糰。以手搓至有彈力。放在塗油瓦盆中，用濕布蓋住發2小時。

餡料—
* 叉燒切小片。
* 將水及調味料傾入小煲內煮沸，生粉水亦流入和勻。加叉燒、葱粒拌成一團雪凍。分成32份候用。

完成—
* 麵糰取出置桌上搓成長條，分切32等份。以木棍輾成圓形，放入一份餡料，收口捏實。以白紙一方墊底，排放焗盤上。置溫暖地方發1小時至鬆身。
* 蛋1只打爛塗在麵包上，放入已開350度（煤氣4度）之焗爐內焗16分鐘至金黃色。取出塗以糖水即成。

Ingredients:

Yeast Paste-
1 tsp dry yeast
1/2 tsp sugar
1/4 cup warm water
3 tbsp high protein flour

Bread Dough-
10 oz (280 g) high protein flour
2 oz (56 g) sugar
1 egg
1 tbsp evaporated milk
1/3 cup warm water
2 tbsp melted butter

Filling-
8 oz (224 g) cha shiu
1/3 cup water
2 tsp oyster sauce
1 tsp sugar
1/8 tsp pepper
1 tsp sesame oil
2 tbsp cornflour mix
2 tbsp chopped chives

Brushing-
1 beaten egg
1/2 cup light syrup

Method:

Yeast Paste-
* Sprinkle the dry yeast and sugar into the warm water. Cover and leave for 10 minutes till frothy. Sift in the flour to mix into a smooth paste. Leave to prove for 10 more minutes.

Bread Dough-
* Sift the high protein flour on to a table to make a well. Put in the sugar, egg, evaporated milk, yeast paste and warm water to mix evenly. Draw in the flour to knead into a soft dough. Add the melted butter to knead thoroughly. Pound until firm then place into a greased mixing bowl and cover with a towel to prove for 2 hours.

Filling-
* Cut the cha shiu into thin pieces.
* Bring the water to boil with the seasoning then blend in the cornflour mix to thicken. Stir in the cha shiu and chives to mix well. Leave to cool and divide into 32 portions.

To Complete-
* Remove the dough and divide into 32 portions. Roll each portion into a round. Put in 1 portion of the filling and draw the edges to seal tightly. Stick a piece of paper on the sealed side. Leave to prove on a greased baking tray for 1 hour.
* Brush the top of each bread with the beaten egg. Bake for 16 minutes in a preheated 350°F (Gas Mark 4) oven till golden brown. Remove and brush with the light syrup.

牛 肉 燒 賣
Beef Shiu My

材料：

餡－牛肉 8 安（224克）
　　馬蹄 2 安（56克）
　　菓皮½方吋
　　葱 1 條
　　羌茸½茶匙

皮－汀麵 4 安（112克）
　　鹽¼茶匙
　　沸水½杯
　　豬油 1 茶匙
　　芫茜點綴

調味－生抽 1 湯匙
　　　生粉 1 茶匙
　　　糖 1 茶匙
　　　酒 1 茶匙
　　　胡椒粉少許
　　　水½杯
　　　油 1 湯匙

製法：

餡－
* 牛肉洗淨抹乾，切成大件。馬蹄去皮切成幼粒。菓皮以熱水浸透剁爛。葱切幼粒與羌茸同放肉機中絞成肉茸。
* 將全部調味料放在碗內拌溶，流入肉茸搞勻。置一旁醃30分鐘。
* 牛肉轉放深桶內撻透留用。

皮－
* 汀麵與鹽同篩在盆內，將沸水沖入快手搞勻。倒置案上蓋着 1 分鐘，加豬油搓成軟糰。

完成－
* 將汀麵糰搓成長條切粒，以木棍開成薄圓形。放入餡料，以手將燒賣捏成窄身之圓柱形。開口處用刀抹平。以芫茜點綴。
* 蒸籠塗油，將燒賣放入以猛火蒸 5 分鐘。

Ingredients:

Filling-
8 oz (224 g) beef
2 oz (56 g) water chestnuts
1/2 sq. in. tangerine peel
1 spring onion
1/2 tsp minced ginger

Pastry-
4 oz (112 g) wheat starch
1/4 tsp salt
1/2 cup boiling water
1 tsp lard
parsley for garnishing

Seasoning-
1 tbsp light soy
1 tsp cornflour
1 tsp sugar
1 tsp wine
1/8 tsp pepper
1/2 cup water
1 tbsp oil

Method:

Filling-
* Wash and dry the beef then cut into chunks. Peel and dice the water chestnuts. Soak the tangerine peel in the hot water till soft and mince. Chop the spring onion. Put all the above ingredients with the ginger into a food processor to mince into a purée.
* Place all the seasoning in a bowl and stir till dissolves. Stream into the beef to mix well. Marinate for 30 minutes.
* Put the beef purée in the mixing bowl to pound until firm.

Pastry-
* Sift the wheat starch and salt in a mixing bowl. Pour in the boiling water and stir vigorously. Cover for 1 minute then add the lard to knead well.

To Complete-
* Roll the dough into a thin long cylinder. Divide into 40 equal portions. Roll each into a small thin round to put in the filling. Press in the edges to shape like a basket. Flatten the top with a knife then garnish with the parlsey.
* Put in a greased steamer to cook over high heat for 5 minutes.

11

白菜餃子
Cabbage Dumplings

材料：

餡—紅蘿蔔 3 安（84克）
　　蝦肉12安（336克）
　　芫茜 2 茶匙

調味—生粉 1 茶匙
　　　胡椒粉½茶匙
　　　糖½茶匙
　　　鹽½茶匙

皮—汀麵 5 安（140克）
　　生粉½安（14克）
　　麵粉½茶匙
　　鹽¼茶匙
　　沸水¾杯
　　豬油½湯匙

綠色水數滴

製法：

餡—
* 紅蘿蔔飛水過冷河，隔乾水份切幼
　粒候用。
* 蝦洗淨切粗粒，加調味料和勻撻至
　爽身。拌入紅蘿蔔粒及芫茜茸。放
　雪櫃內雪 1 小時。

皮—
* 汀麵、生粉、麵粉同篩深盆中，與
　鹽¼茶匙拌勻。沖入沸水快手搞勻
　後，放在桌上搓軟。再加豬油搓成
　一軟糰。

完成—
* 將軟糰搓成長條，分成40等份。每
　份皮用拍皮刀壓成橢圓形，放入餡
　料捏成一棵白菜形，塗以綠色水。
　置塗油蒸籠內中火蒸 6 分鐘即成。

Ingredients:

Filling-
3 oz (84 g) carrot
12 oz (336 g) shelled shrimps
2 tsp chopped parsley

Seasoning-
1 tsp cornflour
1/8 tsp pepper
1/2 tsp sugar
1/2 tsp salt

Pastry-
5 oz (140 g) wheat starch
1/2 oz (14 g) cornflour
1/2 tsp flour
1/4 tsp salt
3/4 cup boiling water
1/2 tbsp lard

1/4 tsp green food colouring

Method:

Filling-
* *Blanch and refresh the carrot. Dice finely for later use.*
* *Dice the shrimps coarsely then blend in the mixed seasoning and pound until firm. Add the diced carrot and parsley to mix thoroughly. Chill in the refrigerator for 1 hour.*

Pastry-
* *Sift the wheat starch, cornflour, flour and salt in a bowl. Pour in the boiling water and stir quickly. Remove on to a table, add the lard to knead into a soft dough.*

To Complete-
* *Roll the dough into a cylinder and divide into 40 equal portions. Press each portion into a round with a pastry knife. Put in the filling and draw the edges to seal and shape as a cabbage. Brush some green colouring on the edge of the pastry. Arrange in a greased steamer to cook for 6 minutes.*

蝦米腸粉

Che Cheung Fun (Ricesheet Rolls)

材料：

粘粉 8 安（224克）
清水 3 杯
粟粉 2 安（56克）
蝦米茸 2 安（56克）
葱粒 3 湯匙

調味－鹽 1 茶匙
　　　糖 ½ 茶匙
　　　生油 1 安（28克）

製法：

* 粘粉加水搞勻放置一旁浸 ½ 小時，再拌入粟粉和勻以篩隔淨。
* 鹽、糖、油一同放入拌勻。
* 腸粉鍋內注水大半鍋燒沸。架上舖上濕薄布一幅，倒入米漿一殼，洒下蝦米及葱粒。
* 蓋上鍋蓋蒸 1－2 分鐘，取出平放在塗油竹架上捲成條。剪開洒上甜醬油及熟油。

Ingredients:

8 oz (224 g) rice flour
3 cups water
2 oz (56 g) cornflour
2 oz (56 g) minced dried shrimps
3 tbsp chopped spring onions

Seasoning-
1 tsp salt
¹/₂ tsp sugar
1 oz (28 g) oil

Method:

* *Sift the flour in a mixing bowl then pour in the water to mix well. Leave aside to soak for 30 minutes then add the cornflour to stir throughly. Filter through a fine sieve.*
* *Season to taste with the salt, sugar and oil.*
* *Half fill the cooker with water then bring it to boil. Line a damped linen on to the rack. Pour 1 scoop of the rice batter on the linen. Sprinkle some dried shrimps and spring onions on top. Cover to cook for 1 to 2 minutes.*
* *Remove the linen with the rice sheet and spread on to a greased bamboo rack with the rice sheet facing down. Gently tear out the linen. Cut and roll the rice sheet into a cylinder then section with a pair of scissors. Serve hot with sweetened soy sauce and oil.*

豉椒鳳爪
Chicken Claws in Black Bean Sauce

材料：

鳳爪 1 磅（½ 公斤）
鹽 1 湯匙
老抽 2 湯匙
沸油 ½ 鑊
水 3 杯
羌 6 片
生葱 3 棵
八角 3 - 4 粒
蒜頭茸 3 粒
豆豉醬 2 湯匙
紅椒 3 隻切粒

調味一酒 1 湯匙
　　　鹽 ¼ 茶匙
　　　糖 2 茶匙
　　　老抽 3 湯匙
　　　胡椒粉、蔴油各少許
　　　生粉水 1 茶匙

製法：

* 鷄爪用鹽擦勻後切去指尖。清洗乾淨飛水隔乾水份。用老抽醃過。每一鷄爪切成 2 至 3 份。放沸油中炸至金黃色。沖洗乾淨。
* 壓力煲加水、羌、葱、八角及鷄爪煮15分鐘。
* 燒紅鑊加油 2 湯匙，爆香蒜頭，豆豉醬及紅椒。再加入鷄爪同炒。讚酒加調味，再煮 5 分鐘，以生粉水埋饎。

Ingredients:

1 lb (¹/₂ kg) chicken claws
1 tbsp salt
¹/₂ wok boiling water
2 tbsp dark soy
¹/₂ wok hot oil
3 cups water
6 pieces ginger
3 chives
4 star anises
3 mashed garlic cloves
2 tbsp black bean paste
3 chillies, diced

Seasoning-
1 tbsp wine
¹/₄ tsp salt
2 tsp sugar
3 tbsp dark soy
¹/₈ tsp pepper
1 tsp sesame oil
1 tsp cornflour mix

Method:

* *Rub the chicken claws with the salt and chop the nails off each claw. Wash thoroughly then blanch in the boiling water for a minute and drain. Brush with the dark soy and chop each claw into 2 to 3 sections. Slowly bring the oil to boil and deep fry the claws till golden brown. Refresh and drain. Keep 2 tbsp oil for later use.*
* *Pour the water into a pressure cooker, add the ginger, chives and star anises to cook with the chicken claws for 15 minutes.*
* *Heat the wok with 2 tbsp oil to sauté the mashed garlic, black bean paste and the diced chillies till fragrant. Put in the chicken claws to sauté thoroughly. Sizzle the wine and season to taste. Add the stock from the pressure cooker then cover to simmer for 5 minutes. Thicken the sauce with the cornflour mix.*

菊 花 酥 餅
Chrysanthemum Crisp

材料：

外皮—麵粉 6 安（168克）
　　　黃色水 $\frac{1}{4}$ 茶匙
　　　水 $\frac{1}{4}$ 杯
　　　豬油 2 安（56克）
內皮—麵粉 4 安（112克）
　　　豬油 2 $\frac{1}{2}$ 安（70克）
餡料—蓮蓉 6 安（168克）

蛋黃 1 隻 塗面
黑芝蔴 $\frac{1}{4}$ 杯裝飾

製法：

外皮—
* 麵粉 6 安篩在桌上開穴。黃色水與
　水和勻倒入穴內與豬油拌勻。然後
　撥入四週之麵粉搓成一軟糰。以毛
　巾蓋住。

內皮—
* 另麵粉 4 安篩在桌上與豬油擦勻成
　一軟糰。

完成—
* 將外內兩軟糰分切24等份，用外皮
　將內皮包住捏緊，全部包妥後以布
　蓋住。
* 以木棍將每個小糰輾成長條，然後
　捲起。再輾成長條又捲起。共捲 3
　次。用棍壓成扁圓形，包入蓮蓉按
　成小餅。用剪刀剪成16小花瓣。將
　每瓣略扭後按薄成菊花形。中央塗
　上蛋黃後再洒芝蔴。放入已開熱至
　350度（煤氣 4 度）之焗爐中焗約15
　至20分鐘。

Ingredients:

Outer Pastry-
6 oz (168 g) plain flour
1/4 tsp yellow food colouring
1/4 cup water
2 oz (56 g) lard

Inner Pastry-
4 oz (112 g) plain flour
2 1/2 oz (70 g) chilled lard

Filling-
6 oz (168 g) lotus seed paste

1 egg yolk for brushing
1/4 cup black sesame seeds

Method:

Outer Pastry-
* *Sift the flour on to the table to
  make a well. Add the colouring
  into the water then pour into the
  well with the lard. Draw in the
  flour to knead into a smooth
  dough. Cover with a towel and
  leave aside.*

Inner Pastry-
* *Sift the flour on to the table and
  add the lard to mix into another
  dough.*

To Complete-
* *Cut both the doughs into 24
  equal portions. Press the outer
  pastry into a round to wrap up
  the inner one. Seal the edges
  tightly.*
* *Press the dough into a long
  strip then roll into a cylinder.
  Give the pastry a turn and repeat
  the rolling method twice. Press
  into a flat round then place a
  piece of lotus paste on it. Draw
  the edges towards the centre to
  seal. Press into a thin piece then
  cut into 16 to 24 petals. Give
  each petal a twist then flatten it.
  Brush the centre with the egg
  yolk and sprinkle the sesame
  seeds on top. Bake in a preheated 350°F (Gas Mark 4) oven
  for 15 to 20 minutes.*

鷄尾飽
Cocktail Bread

材料:

酵種—發子 1½ 茶匙
　　　糖 ½ 茶匙
　　　溫水 ⅓ 杯
　　　筋粉 3 安（84克）
麵糰—筋粉 1 磅（½公斤）
　　　糖 4 安（112克）
　　　蛋 1½ 隻
　　　花奶 1½ 湯匙
　　　溫水 ½ 杯
　　　豬油 2½ 湯匙
餡料—牛油 2½ 安（70克）
　　　糖 3 安（84克）
　　　椰茸 1½ 安（42克）
　　　花奶 2 湯匙
　　　粟粉 1 安（28克）
　　　麵粉 1 安（28克）
　　　香油數滴

製法:

酵種—
* 發子與糖洒在溫水中,以毛巾蓋着發10分鐘。篩入筋粉搞成漿狀。放置一旁發20分鐘。

麵糰—
* 筋粉篩在桌上開穴,放入糖、蛋、奶及水一齊搓匀。再加入酵種搞拌,最後搓入豬油,以手搓至有彈力。放入塗油深盆內,以毛巾蓋着發1½小時。

餡料—
* 牛油與糖同打匀後,加入其他材料拌匀雪實候用。

完成—
* 將麵糰倒在桌上搓成長條,分切24等份。

* 每份麵糰用木棍輾成長方形,放入一份餡料捏妥。置焗盤上以毛巾蓋住發50分鐘。塗上蛋液洒下芝蔴放入已開340度（煤氣4度）焗爐中焗15分鐘。取出塗以糖水即成。

Ingredients:

Yeast Paste-
1¹/₂ tsp dry yeast
¹/₂ tsp sugar
¹/₃ cup warm water
3 oz (84 g) high protein flour

Bread Dough-
1 lb (¹/₂ kg) high protein flour
4 oz (112 g) sugar
1¹/₂ eggs
1¹/₂ tbsp milk
¹/₂ cup warm water
2¹/₂ tbsp melted lard

Filling-
2¹/₂ oz (70 g) butter
3 oz (84 g) sugar
1¹/₂ oz (42 g) desiccated coconut
2 tbsp milk
1 oz (28 g) cornflour

1 oz (28 g) plain flour
¹/₂ tsp vanilla essence

Brushing-
1 beaten egg
¹/₄ cup sesame seeds
¹/₂ cup light syrup

Method:

Yeast Paste-
* Dissolve the dry yeast and sugar in the warm water. Cover to prove for 10 minutes. Sift in the flour to stir into a paste. Prove till frothy.

Bread Dough-
* Sift the flour on to a table and make a well in the centre. Put in the sugar, eggs, milk, water and yeast paste to mix well. Add the melted lard to knead into a soft dough.
* Pound against the table till firm and elastic. Cover and prove in a warm place for 1¹/₂ hours.

Filling-
* Cream the butter and sugar until white. Add all the ingredients to mix into a purée. Chill for later use.

To Complete-
* Divide the dough into portions of 1 oz (28 g) each. Roll each into an oval shape and wrap in the filling. Place on a floured baking tray and prove for another 50 minutes. Brush with the beaten egg and sprinkle with the sesame seeds. Bake in a 340°F (Gas Mark 4) preheated oven for 15 minutes. Remove and brush with the light syrup.

椰茸酥餅
Coconut Crisp

材料：

麵粉 8 安（224克）
梳打粉 1/2 茶匙
發粉 1/2 茶匙
椰茸 2 安（56克）
糖 6 安（168克）
硬豬油 4 安（112克）
蛋 1 隻
蛋黃 2 隻塗面
車厘子 8 粒

製法：

* 麵粉、梳打粉、發粉同篩在桌上。
* 椰茸加在粉料中拌勻開穴。將糖、豬油及蛋同放在穴中搓溶。以手將四週粉料慢慢撥入弄成一軟糰。
* 粉糰搓成長條分切成32等份。每等份搓圓後在中央按一小孔，以 1/4 粒車厘子點綴。塗上一層蛋黃。置已開300度（煤氣2度）之焗爐中焗至金黃色（約15至20分鐘）。

Ingredients:

8 oz (224 g) plain flour
1/2 tsp soda bicarbonate
1/2 tsp baking powder
2 oz (56 g) desiccated coconut
6 oz (168 g) sugar
4 oz (112 g) chilled lard
1 egg
2 egg yolks for brushing
8 cherries

Method:

* Preheat the oven to 300°F (Gas Mark 2).
* Sift the flour, soda and baking powder on to the table. Mix in the desiccated coconut evenly then make a well in the centre.
* Put the sugar, lard and egg in the centre to mix well. Draw in the dry ingredients to work into a soft dough.
* Roll and cut the dough into 32 equal portions. Shape each into a ball then press with your thumb to make a hole in the centre. Put in a quartered cherry and brush the egg yolks on top. Arrange the cookies on a greased baking tray. Bake in the preheated oven for 20 minutes till golden brown.

椰 汁 九 層 糕
Coconut Layer Pudding

材料：

椰汁 6¼ 杯
糖 1½ 杯
鹽 ¼ 茶匙
粘米粉 2¼ 杯
粟粉 ¾ 杯
紅粉水 ½ 茶匙

製法：

* 椰汁放入鍋內，用文火煮熱。即加糖及鹽同熱至完全溶化。
* 將粘米粉及粟粉一同拌入糖水中。用密篩隔去渣滓。
* 將混合物分成 2 等份。其中一份加入紅粉水拌勻。
* 蒸籠內放入已塗油蒸熱之焗盆。倒入 1 杯紅色粉漿蒸10至15分鐘，再蓋上一層白色混合物蒸10至15分鐘。重覆蒸至共九層高。再蒸15分鐘即可。取出攤凍，切成菱形。

Ingredients:

6¼ cups coconut milk
1½ cups sugar
¼ tsp salt
2¼ cups rice flour
¾ cup cornflour
½ tsp red colouring

Method:

* *Pour the coconut milk into a saucepan and scald over low heat. Add the sugar and salt to heat until dissolves.*
* *Sift the rice flour and cornflour in the syrup to mix well. Filter the batter through a fine strainer.*
* *Divide the mixture into 2 equal portions. Add the red colouring to one portion.*
* *Pour the batter into a greased heated tin to steam into a nine layers pudding of alternate colours, starting with 1 cup of the red batter to make a red layer. Allow 10 to 15 minutes cooking time for 1 layer. Remove and leave to cool then cut into diamond shaped pieces.*

椰 汁 年 糕
Coconut New Year Pudding

材料：

馬蹄粉 6 安（168克）
汀麵 4 安（112克）
水 6 杯
椰汁 2 杯
煉奶 1 罐
粘米粉 4 安（112克）
糯米粉 6 安（168克）
糖 1 磅（½公斤）

製法：

* 水 2 杯開馬蹄粉及汀麵。搞勻後加入椰汁、煉奶、再篩入粘米粉、糯米粉拌勻。
* 用餘水 4 杯與糖同放保內煮溶。放至略涼時，把糖水沖入粉水中搞勻。
* 糕盆放蒸籠內，塗油後倒入一亮粉漿蒸 8 分鐘。揭蓋再倒一亮再蒸 8 分鐘。如是重覆數次至蒸完為止。最後一層需蒸 10 分鐘。取出攤凍。

Ingredients:

6 oz (168 g) water chestnut starch
4 oz (112 g) wheat starch
6 cups water
2 cups coconut milk
1 tin condensed milk
4 oz (112 g) rice flour
6 oz (168 g) glutinous rice flour
1 lb (¹/₂ kg) sugar

Method:

* *Soak the water chestnut starch and wheat starch in 2 cups of water. Stir in the coconut milk and condensed milk. Sift in the rice and glutinous rice flour to stir until evenly mixed.*
* *Bring the remaining water to boil in a saucepan. Add the sugar to simmer till dissolved. Leave to cool then pour into the batter to mix thoroughly.*
* *Grease a cake tin and place into the upper tier of the steamers. Pour in 1 scoop of batter to steam for 8 minutes. Repeat scoop by scoop until the batter is finished. The last layer should be steamed for 10 minutes. Remove and leave to cool.*
* *Slice the pudding into small pieces then dip in beaten egg and shallow fry till both sides are golden. Serve hot.*

椰 汁 糖 環
Coconut Rosettes

材料：

麵粉10安（280克）
鷄蛋 3 隻
糖 5 安（140克）
椰汁 1 杯
鮮奶 1 杯
油½鍋

製法：

* 麵粉篩在大盆中。在中央開穴。
* 鷄蛋打爛逐少將糖加入打溶。
* 椰汁與奶混合加入蛋液中同打勻後
  ，慢慢加入麵粉窩中開成稀麵漿。
  放置 1 小時。
* 將糖環模放在油鍋內以中火將油煮
  沸。隨將模取離油鍋輕輕放在粉漿
  上沾上粉糊。放入油中炸至自動退
  出。續炸至金黃色即可撈起。攤凍
  放罐中可保存一至兩個月。

Ingredients:

10 oz (280 g) plain flour
3 eggs
5 oz (140g) sugar
1 cup coconut milk
1 cup fresh milk
¹/2 wok hot oil

Method:

* *Sift the flour into a mixing bowl
  then make a well in the centre.*
* *Whisk the eggs in another mixing bowl till fluffy. Gradually
  beat in the sugar till dissolves.*
* *Mix the coconut milk with the
  milk then stir into the egg batter.
  Pour the batter into a mixing
  bowl to whisk well with the
  flour. Leave for 1 hour to
  mature.*
* *Place the rosette moulds in the
  hot oil and bring to the boil.
  Remove and dip carefully in the
  well stirred batter. Return the
  moulds into the hot oil to deep
  fry till the cakes leave the
  moulds. Continue to deep fry till
  golden brown. Drain and leave
  to cool. The rosettes can be kept
  in an airtight tin for 2 months.*

四色燒賣
4 Colour Shiu My

材料：

餡－上肉 6 安（168克）
　　蝦仁 6 安（168克）
　　羗茸 1 茶匙
　　葱茸 1 茶匙
　　冬瓜 8 安（224克）

調味－鹽 $\frac{1}{4}$ 茶匙
　　　生抽 1 茶匙
　　　酒 1 茶匙

皮 －麵粉 1 磅（ $\frac{1}{2}$ 公斤）
　　　沸水 $\frac{3}{4}$ 杯
　　　凍水 $\frac{1}{2}$ 杯

點綴－ 咸蛋黃茸 2 湯匙
　　　青豆茸 2 湯匙
　　　紅蘿蔔茸 2 湯匙
　　　雲耳茸 2 湯匙

製法：

餡－
* 上肉洗淨，抹乾水份後剁爛成茸。
  以生抽、酒及生粉各 1 茶匙，糖 $\frac{1}{2}$
  茶匙，胡椒粉少許，水 2 湯匙及油
  1 湯匙和勻醃20分鐘。
* 蝦仁洗淨，抹乾水份後切粒，加入
  羗茸、葱茸撈勻。
* 冬瓜用羗磨磨幼，與調味料一同加
  入肉中拌勻。置雪柜內雪 1 小時。

皮－
* 麵粉篩在桌上分成兩份。一份放在
  盆內，加入沸水搞勻成一軟糰；另
  一份在中央開穴，加入凍水搓成軟
  糰。

完成－
* 將兩份軟糰一同搓勻，以手弄成長
  條，分切60等份。
* 以木棍將每一小份軟糰輾平成一小
  圓形，包入餡料，做成四瓣之燒賣
  ，每瓣放入少許咸蛋黃茸、青豆茸
  ，紅蘿蔔茸及雲耳茸。
* 將燒賣排放已塗油蒸籠內，以猛火
  蒸10分鐘即可。

Ingredients:

Filling-
6 oz (168 g) pork loin
6 oz (168 g) shelled shrimps
1 tsp minced ginger
1 tsp chopped chives
8 oz (224 g) winter melon

Seasoning-
1/4 tsp salt
1 tsp light soy
1 tsp wine

Pastry-
1 lb (1/2 kg) plain flour
3/4 cup boiling water
1/2 cup cold water

Garnishing-
2 tbsp minced egg yolk
2 tbsp minced sweet peas
2 tbsp minced carrot
2 tbsp minced black fungus

Method:

Filling-
* Wash, dry and mince the pork loin. Marinate with 1 tsp each of soy, wine and cornflour, 1/2 tsp sugar, 1/8 tsp pepper, 2 tbsp water and 1 tbsp oil for 20 minutes.
* Wash, dry and dice the shelled shrimps then mix well with the ginger and chopped chives.
* Grate the winter melon and mix thoroughly with the pork, shrimps and seasoning. Leave in the refrigerater for 1 hour.

Pastry-
* Sift the plain flour on to the table and divide into 2 portions. Place 1 portion into a mixing bowl and stir well with the boiling water. Make a well in the centre of the remaining portion and knead into a soft dough with the cold water.

To Complete-
* Combine the 2 doughs together and knead into a soft and smooth pastry. Roll the pastry into a cylinder and cut into 60 equal portions.
* Roll each portion into a thin round and put in the filling. Shape each into a shiu my, with 4 cases. Place the egg yolk, sweet peas, carrot and black fungus into each case.
* Arrange the shiu my in a greased steamer and cook over moderate heat for 10 minutes. Remove and serve hot.

肉 丸 粥
Congee with Meatballs

材料：

猪肉10安（280克）
馬蹄 3 粒
米 ½ 杯
腐皮 2 塊
白果10粒
水18杯
羌絲 1 湯匙
芫茜 2 棵

調味一鹽 2 茶匙
　　　胡椒粉 ¼ 茶匙
　　　油 1 湯匙

製法：

* 猪肉洗淨剁爛成茸。以鹽 ¼ 茶匙，
  糖、生抽、酒各 1 茶匙，古月粉少
  許，生粉 2 茶匙，水 3 湯匙，油 2
  茶匙和勻醃30分鐘。用手撻勻放置
  一旁候用。
* 馬蹄剁成茸，放入猪肉內拌勻同撻
  至起膠。
* 米洗淨隔乾水份。以少許鹽、油撈
  勻。
* 腐皮洗淨撕碎。白果去壳去皮。
* 將水10杯放入壓力保內，加米、腐
  皮、白果同煮沸後轉用中火保20分
  鐘。
* 揭蓋加入餘水 8 杯，再煮30分鐘。
* 將肉茸唧成小丸子放入粥內。繼續
  煮 5 分鐘。試妥調味以碗盛起。洒
  上羌絲、芫茜絲即可食用。

Ingredients:

10 oz (280 g) pork
3 water chestnuts
½ cup rice
1 tsp salt
1 tbsp oil
2 bean curd sheets

10 ginkgo nuts
18 cups water
1 tbsp shredded ginger
2 parsley sprigs

Marinade-
1½ tbsp light soy
1 tbsp cornflour
1 tbsp sugar
1 tsp wine
3 tbsp water
2 tsp oil

Seasoning-
2 tsp salt
¼ tsp pepper
1 tbsp oil

Method:

* *Wash and mince the pork. Soak in the marinade and leave aside for 30 minutes. Pound until springy.*
* *Mince the water chestnuts and stir into the pork then pound again till firm.*
* *Wash and drain the rice. Mix well with the salt and oil.*
* *Wash and tear the bean curd sheets into pieces. Shell and peel the ginkgo nuts.*
* *Put 10 cups of the water into a pressure cooker. Pour in the rice, bean curd sheets and ginkgo nuts to bring to the boil. Cook for 20 minutes till the rice is soft.*
* *Remove the lid, add the remaining water and continue to boil for ½ hour without the lid on.*
* *Shape the minced pork into small balls and drop into the congee. Continue to boil for 5 minutes. Season to taste. Serve hot with the shredded ginger and parsley.*

33

瑤 柱 齋 粥

Congee with Scallops

材料：

米½杯
腐皮 2 塊（隨意）
白果10粒（隨意）
水16杯
江瑤柱 2 安（56克）

調味－鹽 2½ 茶匙

製法：

* 米洗淨後隔乾水份。用油 1 湯匙，鹽 1 茶匙拌勻。
* 腐皮略洗後撕碎。
* 白果去売浸於熱水中約10分鐘後去衣。
* 深鍋 1 隻洗淨，將水16杯放入大火煮沸。隨即把腐皮，白果及米放入，以中火續煮30分鐘。
* 瑤柱略洗後以沸水浸 1 小時。取出撕幼，加入沸粥內煮 1½ 小時至滑為止。食時配以各式小菜。

Ingredients:

1/2 cup rice
1 tbsp oil
1 tsp salt
2 bean curd sheets
10 ginkgo nuts
2 cups hot water
16 cups water
2 oz (56 g) dried scallops

Seasoning-
21/2 tsp salt

Method:

* *Wash and drain the rice then mix with the oil and salt.*
* *Wash and tear the bean curd sheets into small pieces.*
* *Shell and immerse the ginkgo nuts in 1/2 cup of the hot water for 10 minutes. Peel off the skin.*
* *Put the water into a saucepan to boil over high heat. Pour in the bean curd sheets, nuts and rice and continue to cook over medium heat for 30 minutes.*
* *Wash and soak the scallops in the remaining hot water for 1 hour. Remove and shred finely. Pour into the congee to boil for 1 1/2 hours until smooth and tender. Serve with savoury dishes.*

豬什粥
Congee with Pork Offals

材料：

米½杯
白果20粒
腐皮 2 塊
水20杯
豬肝 4 安（112克）
豬腰 4 安（112克）
豬肚 4 安（112克）
豬心 4 安（112克）
羌絲 2 湯匙
葱絲 2 湯匙
芫茜 2 棵修妥
油條 2 條

調味－鹽 2 茶匙
　　　胡椒粉少許
　　　蔴油 1 湯匙

製法：

* 米洗淨後以油 1 湯匙，鹽 1 茶匙和勻。放置一旁候用。
* 白果去壳去衣。腐皮洗淨撕成小片。
* 深鍋中放水20杯煮沸。加入米、白果、腐皮，以中火煮 2 小時。調妥味。
* 豬什洗淨切片，以生粉、羌汁、酒醃 1 小時。取出用沸水略浸後轉浸於冰水中。隔去水份，再以生粉、胡椒粉及生抽捞勻。
* 大碗中放入蔴油及豬什，將沸粥倒入。洒上羌葱絲及芫茜。配以油條，即可食用。

Ingredients:

½ cup rice
20 ginkgo nuts
2 bean curd sheets
20 cups water
4 oz (112 g) pig's liver
4 oz (112 g) pig's kidney
4 oz (112 g) pig's stomach
4 oz (112 g) pig's heart
2 tbsp shredded ginger
2 shredded spring onions
2 parsley sprigs, trimmed
2 twisted doughnuts

Seasoning-
2 tsp salt
¼ tsp pepper
1 tbsp sesame oil

Method:

* Wash and season the rice with 1 tbsp oil and 1 tsp salt. Leave aside for later use.
* Shell and peel the ginkgo nuts. Wash and break the bean curd sheets into small pieces.
* Bring the water to boil in a saucepan. Pour in the rice, ginkgo nuts and bean curd sheets to simmer for 2 hours over medium heat. Season to taste.
* Wash and slice the liver, kidney, stomach and heart. Marinate with 1½ tbsp each of cornflour, ginger juice and wine for 1 hour. Scald, refresh and soak in the iced water. Drain and marinate again with some cornflour, pepper and light soy.
* Place the offal slices into a serving bowl and add the sesame oil. Pour in the boiling congee then sprinkle the ginger, spring onions and parsley on top. Serve with the twisted doughnuts.

椰 汁 鷄 蛋 卷
Crackling Egg Rolls

材料：

蛋 4 隻
糖 4 安（112克）
椰汁 $\frac{1}{4}$ 杯
生粉 2 安（56克）
筋粉 1 安（28克）
臭粉 $\frac{1}{8}$ 茶匙
梳打粉 $\frac{1}{8}$ 茶匙

製法：

* 蛋逐隻打入蛋桶中，一直打至鬆軟浮起。加入糖、椰汁同打勻。
* 將生粉、筋粉篩入桶中，加臭粉、梳打粉和勻。
* 蛋挾燒熱，以合桃肉一片擦勻，倒入 1 湯匙蛋混合物。夾上蛋挾，每邊烘約 6 至 8 秒鐘。
* 揭開蛋挾，以小刀及筷子沿邊捲起成筒形。攤凍放入瓶內。

Ingredients:

4 eggs
4 oz (112 g) sugar
1/4 cup coconut milk
2 oz (56 g) cornflour
1 oz (28 g) high protein flour
1/8 tsp ammonia soda
1/8 tsp soda bicarbonate

Method:

* Beat the eggs in a mixing bowl until fluffy. Add the sugar and coconut milk to beat until the sugar dissolves.
* Sift the cornflour and high protein flour into the mixing bowl. Add the ammonia soda and soda bicarbonate to mix evenly with the batter.
* Heat and grease the crackling egg mould with a piece of walnut. Pour in 1 tbsp of the batter and sandwich it to toast for 6 to 8 seconds on each side.
* Open and roll the biscuit with the help of a knife and a chopstick. Leave to cool and keep in an airtight tin.

牛肉角仔
Crackling Triangles

材料：

春卷皮 4 安（112克）
免治牛肉 6 安（168克）
葱頭茸 1 湯匙
蒜頭茸 1 茶匙
洋葱茸 3 湯匙
紅椒茸 1 茶匙
羌茸 1 茶匙
蛋白 $\frac{1}{2}$ 隻

調味一酒 1 茶匙
　　　鹽 $\frac{1}{6}$ 茶匙
　　　糖 $\frac{1}{2}$ 茶匙
　　　五香粉 1 茶匙
　　　紅椒粉 1 茶匙
　　　黑椒粉 $\frac{1}{4}$ 茶匙

製法：

* 春卷皮剪成長條約 $1\frac{1}{4}$ 吋（3公分）闊
  候用。
* 免治牛肉用生抽 1 湯匙、生粉、糖
  各 1 茶匙、酒 $\frac{1}{2}$ 茶匙、水 3 湯匙和
  勻醃 $\frac{1}{2}$ 小時。
* 燒紅鑊加油少許，爆葱、蒜頭，加
  入洋葱炒香。
* 另起鑊爆香紅椒及羌茸，倒入牛肉
  炒至乾水，將已爆之葱、蒜各茸同
  加入拌炒。讚酒加入全部調味後，
  試味盛起攤凍。以春卷皮包成小三
  角形。用蛋白收口。
* 燒油半鍋至大熱時即將角仔放入炸
  至金黃色。

Ingredients:

4 oz (112 g) spring roll pastry
6 oz (168 g) minced beef
2 tbsp oil
1 tbsp minced shallot
1 tsp minced garlic
3 tbsp chopped onion

1 tsp chopped red chillies
1 tsp minced ginger
$\frac{1}{2}$ egg white
$\frac{1}{2}$ wok oil

Marinade-
1 tbsp light soy
1 tsp cornflour
1 tsp sugar
$\frac{1}{2}$ tsp wine
3 tbsp water

Seasoning-
1 tsp wine
$\frac{1}{6}$ tsp salt
$\frac{1}{2}$ tsp sugar
1 tsp five spice powder
1 tsp paprika
$\frac{1}{4}$ tsp black pepper

Method:

* Cut the spring roll pastry into
  long strips of about $1\frac{1}{4}$" (3 cm)
  wide.
* Soak the minced beef in the
  mixed marinade and leave for 30
  minutes.
* Heat the wok with 1 tbsp of oil to
  sauté the shallot, garlic and
  onion till pungent. Remove.
* Heat another wok with the
  remaining oil to sauté the chillies
  and ginger. Pour in the minced
  beef to fry until dry. Return the
  sautéed shallot, garlic and onion
  into the wok. Sizzle the wine and
  season to taste. Remove and
  leave aside to cool. Place a tsp of
  the filling at one end of the pastry strip and wrap into a small
  triangle. Seal tightly with the egg
  white.
* Bring the oil to boil and deep fry
  the triangles till golden brown.
  Remove and drain on absorbent
  paper.

茶 泡

Crispy Munchies

材料：

蠶豆 6 安（168克）
花生 6 安（168克）
慈菇 6 安（168克）
薯仔 6 安（168克）
芋頭 6 安（168克）
鹽粉 1 湯匙

製法：

* 蠶豆以沸水浸發24小時，去皮後再
  放沸鹽水中煮片刻。取出攤凍。
* 花生用沸鹽水浸數小時去皮，隔清
  水吹乾。
* 慈菇、薯仔、芋頭皆去皮切薄片，
  截成欖核形或長方小片。以沸鹽水
  浸片刻後冲淨。
* 將以上各物分別放沸油鍋中炸至金
  黃色。撈起隔淨餘油。洒以鹽粉，
  攤凍後放瓶中蓋密。

Ingredients:

6 oz (168 g) broad beans
3 cups hot water
6 oz (168 g) peanuts
6 oz (168 g) arrowroot
3 cups boiling salted water
6 oz (168 g) new potatoes
6 oz (168 g) taro
4 cups oil
1 tbsp fine salt

Method:

* *Soak the broad beans in the hot
  water for 24 hours and peel off
  the skin. Remove and put into
  the boiling salted water to simmer for 3 minutes. Drain and
  leave to cool.*
* *Soak the peanuts in the same hot
  salted water for a few hours and
  peel. Drain and leave to dry.*
* *Peel and slice the arrowroot,
  new potatoes and taro. Cut into
  diamond shapes or small
  rectangles as desired. Soak all
  these in the hot salted water for
  15 minutes then refresh and
  drain.*
* *Gently bring the oil to boil and
  deep fry all the above ingredients
  in the hot oil until golden and
  crisp. Drain and sprinkle the
  fine salt evenly on the ingredients. Leave to cool then store
  in an airtight container. Serve as
  a snack.*

琉璃金棗
Crystal Date Jam Spirals

材料：

糯米粉 8 安（224克）
沸水 ½ 杯
薯仔 1 磅（½ 公斤）
棗茸 8 安（224克）
水 1 杯
糖 1 杯

製法：

* 糯米粉篩入大盆中，將沸水慢慢冲
  入搞勻。
* 薯仔焓熟去皮，夾成薯茸加入糯米
  粉中，用力搓勻。分成等份，用手
  按成薄圓形。
* 將棗茸放入粉皮中，捏緊後搓至兩
  頭尖。
* 燒油 ½ 鑊，油將沸時倒入金棗炸片
  刻撈出。再將油煮沸，將金棗倒入
  ，上色後改用文火炸片刻。倒起隔
  去油。
* 水 1 杯放鍋中加糖 1 杯同煮至濃，
  加油 1 湯匙，以鏟和勻。倒入金棗
  滾勻。轉放塗滿油之碟中個別分開
  。

Ingredients:

8 oz (224 g) glutinous rice flour
½ cup boiling water
1 lb (½ kg) potatoes
8 oz (224 g) date jam
½ wok oil
1 cup water
1 cup sugar

Method:

* *Sift the rice flour into a mixing
  bowl. Gradually pour in the
  boiling water to stir till well
  mixed.*
* *Cook, peel and mash the
  potatoes. Mix with the glutinous
  rice flour and knead into a soft
  dough. Divide into 32 equal portions. Press with your palm to
  form a round pastry.*
* *Divide the date jam into 32 equal
  portions and place 1 portion in
  the centre of the pastry. Wrap up
  tightly then shape into a spiral.*
* *Bring the oil to just boil in a
  clean wok. Deep fry the spirals
  till golden then remove and
  drain. Heat the oil again to deep
  fry the spirals for a second time.
  Remove and drain on absorbent
  paper. Leave 1 tbsp oil for later
  use.*
* *Bring 1 cup of water and sugar
  to boil in another wok. Simmer
  until a thick syrup is formed.
  Add the oil to stir with the syrup.
  Slide in the spirals to coat
  evenly. Transfer to a greased
  platter.*

空 心 煎 堆

Deep Fried Sesame Balls

材料：

糯米粉10安（280克）
水 ¾ 杯
沙糖 4½ 安（126克）
芝蔴 1 杯
炸油 ½ 鑊

製法：

* 糯米粉篩在桌上開穴，將水與糖放入穴中。
* 穴中水及糖以手拌勻，慢慢將四週之粉撥入搓成軟糰。
* 粉糰搓成長圓柱形，對切成等份。共切為40粒小麵糰。以手掌搓成圓球形。放在芝蔴上滾滿一層芝蔴。
* 油大半鍋中火燒沸。停火將小圓球放入炸至浮起時，再轉中火續炸。以煎堆鏟按至圓球膨脹發大，炸至金黃色時即可撈起。

Ingredients:

10 oz (280 g) glutinous rice flour
³/4 cup water
4¹/2 oz (126 g) sugar
1 cup sesame seeds for coating
¹/2 wok oil

Method:

* *Sift the glutinous rice flour on to the table. Make a well in the centre to put in the water and sugar.*
* *Dissolve the sugar in the water then gradually work in the flour to knead into a smooth dough.*
* *Roll the dough into a cylinder and cut into 40 equal portions. Shape each portion into a ball then coat with the sesame seeds.*
* *Heat the oil until very hot then turn off the heat and put in the sesame balls. When the balls begin to float, turn on medium heat. Press each ball with a ladle until it has inflated.*
* *Continue to deep fry the balls till golden brown. Remove and drain on absorbent paper.*

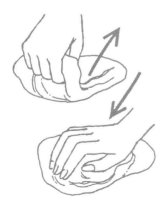

鴨 絲 盆 粉

Diced Pudding with Roast Duck

材料：

盆粉—粘米粉10安（280克）
　　　鹽2茶匙
　　　味精$\frac{1}{2}$茶匙
　　　鹼水$\frac{1}{2}$茶匙
　　　水3$\frac{1}{2}$杯
　　　油$\frac{1}{4}$杯

配料—燒鴨6安（168克）
　　　青菜4安（112克）
　　　羌2片
　　　葱頭1粒

調味—酒1茶匙
　　　上湯4杯
　　　鹽$\frac{1}{2}$茶匙
　　　生抽1茶匙
　　　糖1茶匙

製法：

盆粉—

* 粘粉篩在盆中，加入鹽、味精、鹼水及水和成米漿。再加油拌勻。轉倒入塗油糕盆內，放蒸籠中隔水蒸10分鐘，至三成熟時，以木棒搞拌，再蒸10分鐘。又搞一次。共搞三次使成爽口之糕。蓋上鑊蓋，再蒸30分鐘。取出攤凍，切成四方或菱形之盆粉粒。

配料—

* 燒鴨拆肉切絲，青菜洗淨摘妥，羌切絲。葱頭拍扁。
* 燒紅鑊，放油2湯匙煮沸爆香羌葱頭，灒酒傾下上湯，加調味煮沸後，倒入盆粉、燒鴨及青菜煮片刻。盛起上桌。

Ingredients:

Pudding-
10 oz (280 g) rice flour
2 tsp salt
1/2 tsp M.S.G.
1/2 tsp alkali water
3 1/2 cups water
1/4 cup oil

Others-
6 oz (168 g) roast duck
4 oz (112 g) green vegetables
2 slices ginger
1 shallot
2 tbsp oil

Seasoning-
1 tsp wine
4 cups stock
1/2 tsp salt
1 tsp light soy
1 tsp sugar

Method:

Pudding-
* *Sift the rice flour into a mixing bowl then add the salt, M.S.G., alkali water and water to mix well. Finally blend in the oil to stir thoroughly. Place the batter into a greased cake mould to steam for 10 minutes till 30% cooked. Remove the lid and stir vigorously. Cover to cook for another 10 minutes. Repeat the stirring method 3 times. Cover the lid to cook for another 30 minutes. Remove to cool and cut into rectangular or diamond shape pieces.*

To Complete-
* *Debone and shred the roast duck. Wash and trim the vegetables. Shred the ginger. Mash the shallot.*
* *Heat the wok to bring the oil to boil. Sauté the ginger and shallot till fragrant. Sizzle the wine, pour in the stock and season to taste. Put in the pudding, roast duck and vegetables to cook for a while. Scoop into the bowls and serve hot.*

光 酥 餅
Egg White Cakes

材料：

麵種 4 安（112克）
溫水 ½ 杯
麵粉 10安（280克）
糖 5 安（140克）
溶豬油 2 湯匙
蛋白 2 隻
鮮奶 1 湯匙
發粉 1 茶匙

製法：

* 麵種放在溫水內以手搓勻成漿狀。篩入麵粉和成一軟糰。以濕布蓋住發 8 至12小時。

* 將發至雙倍大之麵糰取出，放置已洒粉之桌上，加入糖、豬油、蛋白，鮮奶及發粉一同搓勻。放置一旁再發 1 小時。

* 將發安之麵糰搓成長條，分切等份（大小隨意）。以手捏成小圓餅。

* 焗盤洒粉，將小圓餅排放入內，置已開定 200 度（煤氣¼度）之慢火焗爐中焗約15分鐘。取出攤凍即成。

Ingredients:

4 oz (112 g) yeast dough
½ cup warm water
10 oz (280 g) flour
5 oz (140 g) sugar
2 tbsp melted lard
2 egg whites
1 tbsp fresh milk
1 tsp baking powder

Method:

* *Place the yeast dough in the warm water to stir thoroughly into a paste. Sift in the flour and knead into a soft dough. Cover with a wet towel and leave to prove for 8 to 12 hours.*

* *Remove the proved dough on to the floured table. Add the sugar, lard, egg whites, milk and baking powder to knead evenly. Dust with some extra flour constantly. Leave aside to prove for 1 hour.*

* *Roll the dough into a cylinder and divide into 8 to 16 equal portions. Press into small round cakes.*

* *Arrange the cakes on to a floured baking tray. Place into a preheated 200°F (Gas Mark ¼) oven to bake for 15 minutes. Remove on a rack and leave to cool.*

動 物 餅 仔
Fish and Piggy Cookies

材料：

麵粉1磅（½公斤）
糖膠1杯
生油½杯
梘水½茶匙
蛋黃3隻

製法：

* 麵粉篩在桌上開穴。將糖膠、生油梘水及蛋黃倒入，慢慢將四週麵粉撥入搓成粉糰。

* 將麵糰搓成長條，分切為2等份。一份分切為1½安（42克）之小麵糰，按入已洒粉之豬仔餅印中。敲出排放在餅盤中。

* 另一份麵糰分切2½安（70克）之小糰，按在魚仔餅印中敲出，排放在另一餅盤中。塗上蛋液。

* 以噴水壺噴水在餅上後，放入 250度（煤氣½度）焗爐焗5分鐘。取出塗以剩餘蛋液，放回爐中，將火開至300度（煤氣2度）焗15分鐘，取出攤凍。

Ingredients:

1 lb (¹/2 kg) plain flour
1 cup syrup
¹/2 cup oil
¹/2 tsp alkali water
3 beaten egg yolks

Method:

* *Preheat the oven to 250°F (Gas Mark ¹/2).*
* *Sift the flour on to the table and make a well in the centre. Put in the syrup, oil, alkali water and 2 egg yolks to mix well. Draw in the flour gradually and knead into a soft dough.*
* *Roll the dough into a cylindrical shape and divide into 2 equal portions. Cut each portion into small doughs weighing 1¹/2 oz (42 g) each. Dust a little flour in the piggy cookie mould. Press the dough into the mould to flatten. Knock the cookies out and place on a floured baking tray.*
* *Cut the remaining dough into portions of 2¹/2 oz (70 g) for the fish cookies. Repeat the procedure as for the piggy cookies.*
* *Spray some water on the cookies and arrange the trays in the middle rack of the preheated oven to bake for 5 minutes. Brush each cookie with the remaining egg yolk then return the tray in the oven and increase the heat to 300°F (Gas Mark 2) to bake for 15 minutes. Remove and leave to cool.*

蘿蔔酥餅
Flaky Cakes with Ham and Turnip

材料：

外皮— 麵粉 5 安（140克）
　　　溫水½杯
內皮— 麵粉 5 安（140克）
　　　豬油 3 安（84克）
餡料— 火腿 5 安（140克）
　　　蘿蔔 8 安（224克）
　　　葱粒 3 湯匙
　　　鹽¼茶匙
　　　糖½茶匙
　　　五香粉 1 茶匙
　　　胡椒粉少許

製法：

外皮—
* 　將外皮用之麵粉篩在桌上開穴，倒入溫水搓成軟糰。
內皮—
* 　另將麵粉 5 安（140克）篩在桌上與豬油輕輕按勻。
* 　將外皮與內皮各搓成長條分切12等份。把外皮按扁包入內皮，壓緊邊沿用木棍輾成長條，然後捲起。重覆一次。即共捲二次，再將皮按薄捏成圓窩形。
餡料—
* 　火腿切茸。蘿蔔去皮洗淨刨絲，加少許鹽醃片刻後，將水份揸乾。火腿茸、蘿蔔絲、葱粒，加調味料撈勻候用。
完成—
* 　餡料分成12等份。放在皮上捏邊收口。將收口處向下放。以手掌按平至約¼吋（½厘米）厚。
* 　燒紅平底鑊，加油少許。將酥餅放入慢火烘至兩邊金黃即可。

Ingredients:

Outer Pastry-
5 oz (140 g) plain flour
1/3 cup warm water

Inner Pastry-
5 oz (140 g) plain flour
3 oz (84 g) chilled lard

Filling-
5 oz (140 g) ham
8 oz (224 g) turnip
3 tbsp diced chives
1/4 tsp salt
1/2 tsp sugar
1 tsp five spice powder
1/8 tsp pepper

Method:

Outer Pastry-
* *Sift the flour on to the table and make a well in the centre. Add the warm water to knead into a smooth dough.*

Inner Pastry-
* *Sift the other portion of flour on the table and lightly press into a soft dough with the lard.*
* *Roll and cut both the doughs into 12 equal portions. Flatten each outer pastry and wrap in a piece of the inner one. Carefully flatten into a long thin strip then roll up. Turn and repeat once. Press it into a flat round.*

Filling-
* *Mince the ham. Peel, wash and shred the turnip. Marinate with a little salt then squeeze out the excess water. Mix all the ingredients with the seasoning.*

To Complete-
* *Divide the filling into 12 equal portions. Wrap each portion with a piece of pastry then draw the edges together to seal securely. Flatten to about 1/4 inch (0.6 cm) thick with the sealed edge facing down.*
* *Heat and grease a griddle to shallow fry the cakes over low heat until both sides are golden. Serve hot.*

鷄蛋泡仔

Fluffy Egg Puffs

材料：

蛋 8 隻
糖 5 安（140 克）
奶水 2 湯匙
香油 1/4 茶匙
自發粉 5 安（140 克）
栗粉 1 安（28 克）
鹽 1/8 茶匙
溶牛油 4 湯匙

製法：

* 蛋與糖同放桶中打至輕軟。將奶水
  及香油逐少加入打勻。
* 自發粉、栗粉及鹽一同篩在紙上，
  慢慢倒入蛋液中以手撈勻。溶牛油
  跟著沖入拌妥。放置片刻待用。
* 鐵模燒紅，以油布逐個抹勻，然後
  將蛋液以匙盛在每個模中約 6 分滿
  。將模合攏以中火每邊燒約 3 分鐘
  。揭開以鐵針或叉挑出排放碟上。

Ingredients:

8 eggs
5 oz (140 g) sugar
2 tbsp milk
1/4 tsp vanilla essence
5 oz (140 g) self raising flour
1 oz (28 g) cornflour
1/8 tsp salt
4 tbsp melted butter

Method:

* *Beat the eggs and sugar in a mixing bowl until light and fluffy. Gradually drop in the milk and vanilla essence to stir well.*
* *Sift the self raising flour, cornflour and salt on a piece of paper then slide into the batter to mix evenly. Blend in the melted butter to fold thoroughly till a smooth batter is formed.*
* *Grease and heat the cake mould till very hot. Spoon in the batter to fill the individual moulds to about 60% full. Close the mould tightly and heat each side for 2 to 3 minutes over moderate heat. Open and remove with a skewer or fork. Arrange on a platter and serve with tea or coffee.*

芝蔴湯丸
Glutinous Rice Balls in Sesame Soup

材料：

皮一糯米 1 磅（½ 公斤）
　　水 2 至 3 杯
　　豬油 1 湯匙

餡一花生醬 ¼ 杯
　　糖 ¼ 杯

糖水一芝蔴糊 8 杯
　　薑 1 片

製法：

皮一
* 糯米洗淨浸40分鐘。隔乾水份，加水磨成粉漿。
* 漿料放在布袋以重物壓乾水份。

餡一
* 花生醬 ¼ 杯與糖 ¼ 杯和勻作餡用。

完成一
* 取出粉料加豬油搓成一軟滑粉糰。
* 將粉糰分切成等份小圓球，每一份按成一小圓餅形，放入花生醬收口捏回一小圓球，置沸水中煮至浮起。
* 芝蔴糊煮沸，加薑及湯丸同煮片刻，用小碗盛起熱食。

Ingredients:

Pastry-
1 lb (¹/₂ kg) glutinous rice
3 cups water
1 tbsp lard

Filling-
¹/₄ cup peanut butter
¹/₄ cup sugar
¹/₂ wok boiling water for blanching

Sweet Soup-
8 cups sweet black sesame soup
1 slice ginger

Method:

Pastry-
* *Wash, rinse and soak the glutinous rice for 40 minutes. Drain and add the water to grind until a smooth batter is formed.*
* *Place the batter into a muslin bag and put a heavy weight on top to drain off the excess water.*

Filling-
* *Mix the peanut butter with the sugar.*

To Complete-
* *Remove the flour from the bag, add the lard to knead into a smooth dough.*
* *Divide the dough into equal portions and press each into a small round. Fill each round with the peanut butter then wrap up to form a small ball. Parboil in the boiling water till they float.*
* *Bring the sweet soup to the boil. Add the ginger and glutinous rice balls to simmer for a while. Serve hot in small bowls.*

韮菜饊餅
Green Leek Swirls

60

材料：

皮—麵粉10安（280克）
　　水¾杯
　　鹽½茶匙

餡—豬肉10安（280克）
　　韮菜粒1杯
　　羌茸1茶匙
　　五香粉1茶匙
　　甜醬1茶匙

製法：

皮—
* 麵粉篩在桌上開穴，加水及鹽和勻成一軟糰。

餡—
* 豬肉剁爛，用胡椒粉少許、生抽、酒及生粉各1茶匙，老抽、糖及蔴油各½茶匙和勻醃10分鐘。再加入其他配料搞成肉醬。

完成—
* 將麵糰分作6至8份。洒少許生粉在桌上。以木棍將麵糰輾成長三角形。餡料攤放在上，由尖處向外捲起捏緊。然後將麵糰豎起在左掌上，以右手掌壓扁成圓餅。
* 平底鍋或鐵板塗油，將餅放在上面煎片刻，至兩面金黃色即成。

Ingredients:

Pastry-
10 oz (280 g) flour
3/4 cup water
1/2 tsp salt

Filling-
10 oz (280 g) pork
1 cup chopped leeks
1 tsp mashed ginger
1 tsp five spice powder
1 tsp Hoi Sin paste

Marinade-
1 tbsp light soy
1/2 tbsp cornflour
1/2 tbsp sugar
1 tsp wine
1/2 tsp dark soy
1/2 tsp sesame oil
1/8 tsp pepper

Method:

Pastry-
* *Sift the flour on to a table and make a well in the centre. Pour in the water and salt then draw in the flour to knead into a soft dough.*

Filling-
* *Clean and mince the pork, immerse in the marinade and leave to stand for 10 minutes. Stir in the other ingredients to mix into a purée.*

To Complete-
* *Divide the dough into 8 portions. Dust the table with some flour then roll each portion into a thin long strip. Spread the meat purée evenly on the surface. Roll up into a cylinder from the narrowest end. Place it vertically on your left palm and press down with the right one. Twist the palms in opposite directions to form a flattened swirl.*
* *Grease a griddle with oil and arrange the swirls to shallow fry till both sides are golden brown. Serve hot.*

薄皮蝦餃
Har Kow (Shrimp Dumpling)

材料：

皮一汀麵 4 安（112 克）
　　　生粉 1 湯匙
　　　沸水 ½ 杯
　　　豬油 1 茶匙
餡一蝦肉 10 安（280 克）
　　　笋 1 安（28 克）
　　　蛋白 ½ 隻

調味一 鹽 ½ 茶匙
　　　　糖 ½ 茶匙
　　　　胡椒粉少許
　　　　生粉 1 茶匙
　　　　蔴油 ½ 茶匙

製法：

皮一
* 汀麵與生粉同篩在大盆中待用。
* 沸水沖入盆中，迅速以木棍搞勻，倒轉在桌上放 1 分鐘。
* 取出加豬油搓勻。搓成幼長條分切 40 小粒。

餡一
* 蝦肉切粒，笋可切幼絲。一同放在大盆中，加入蛋白及調味品。最後落生粉和勻撻至起膠。放雪柜雪 ½ 小時。

完成一
* 將麵粒用拍皮刀壓在桌邊，開成圓形。
* 用竹片挑少許餡放在一邊，然後捏成蝦餃形。
* 蒸籠塗油放入蝦餃。中火蒸 5 分鐘即成。

Ingredients:

Pastry-
4 oz (112 g) wheat starch
1 tbsp cornflour
$1/2$ cup boiling water
1 tsp lard

Filling-
10 oz (280 g) shelled shrimps
1 oz (28 g) carrot
$1/2$ egg white

Seasoning-
$1/2$ tsp salt
$1/2$ tsp sugar
$1/8$ tsp pepper
1 tsp cornflour
$1/2$ tsp sesame oil

Method:

Pastry-
* *Sift the wheat starch and cornflour into a mixing bowl then pour in the boiling water to stir vigorously. Cover for 1 minute and add the lard to knead into a soft dough.*

Filling-
* *Wash and cut each shrimp into three sections. Shred the carrot finely. Place all the ingredients into a bowl. Add the egg white and seasoning to pound until firm. Keep in the refrigerator for 30 minutes.*

To Complete-
* *Cut the dough into 40 equal portions. Roll each portion into a small round. Place the filling on the round and wrap up with 6 pleats on one side forming a bonnet shaped dumpling.*
* *Arrange the Har Kow into a greased steamer over boiling water. Cook over medium heat for 5 minutes. Remove and serve hot.*

賀壽大飽
Long Life Buns

材料：

皮—溫水 1¼ 杯
　　發子 2 茶匙
　　糖½ 茶匙
　　麵粉 1 磅（½ 公斤）
　　發粉 2 茶匙
　　沙糖 2 安（56克）
　　溶豬油 3 湯匙
　　紅粉水 1 湯匙

餡—蓮蓉12安（336克）

製法：

皮—
* 將溫水倒在大碗中，洒入發子及糖，以濕布蓋住發10分鐘。
* 麵粉篩在桌上開穴，將發子水倒入穴中。撥入麵粉慢慢以手和成一軟糰，放在塗油之大盆中，以半濕毛巾蓋住發4小時。取出倒在洒妥粉培之桌上。
* 將發起麵糰略搓後，加入發粉，沙糖與豬油同搓至軟滑。如太濕可逐少加入粉培和勻。

完成—
* 將麵糰搓成圓長條，分切48等份，蓮蓉亦分成48等份。以手將麵糰捏成小窩放入一份蓮蓉後收口。再用手掌將包之一邊捏搓成尖長形。以小刀壓一深紋在中央，使成桃子形。白紙一方貼在包底，排放入蒸籠內，以大火蒸8分鐘即可取出。以乾淨牙刷沾紅粉水，彈在包子上使成小紅點。

Ingredients:

Pastry-
1 1/4 cup warm water
2 tsp dry yeast
1/2 tsp sugar
1 lb (1/2 kg) flour
2 tsp baking powder
2 oz (56 g) fine sugar
3 tbsp melted lard
1 cup flour for dusting
1 tbsp red food colouring

Filling-
12 oz (336 g) sweet lotus seed paste

Method:

Pastry-
* *Pour the warm water into a mixing bowl and scatter in the dry yeast and sugar. Cover and leave for 10 minutes till frothy.*
* *Sift the flour on to the table and make a well in the centre. Pour in the yeast mix and gradually draw in the flour to knead into a soft dough. Place into a greased bowl, cover to prove for 4 hours. Remove on to a floured table.*
* *Add the baking powder, sugar and lard into the dough and mix until smooth. Dust with the flour to knead into a soft dough.*

To Complete-
* *Knead the dough into a long roll and divide into 48 equal portions. Press each portion into a round to wrap in the filling. Draw the edges to seal tightly. Shape one side of the bun into a sharp point and press a deep line from the centre to the point. Flatten the bottom on a sheet of paper. Arrange into a steamer and leave to prove for 10 to 20 minutes. Steam over high heat for 8 minutes then remove.*
* *Dip a stiff-haired tooth-brush in red food colouring. Hold the brush facing up in one hand. Draw a blunt knife across the bristles towards you and spray the colour away from you over the pointed half of the bun. This should result in fine red dots on the buns.*

杧果西米凍
Mango and Sago Pudding

材料：

西米 4 安（112克）
杧果 2 個
大菜 ¾ 安（21克）
水 5 ½ 杯
糖 8 安（224克）
鮮奶 1 杯
蛋 3 只

製法：

* 西米放在 3 杯沸水中煮至透明。置
  筲箕中用水喉冲凍浸住候用。
* 杧果去皮切粒候用。
* 大菜預先浸軟。水 5 ½ 杯倒在鍋內
  煮沸後，將大菜及糖放入文火煮溶
  。
* 大菜水離火後將鮮奶加入和勻。
* 蛋打爛將西米杧果粒拌入和勻。再
  加入大菜糖水中。坐在冰上搞拌至
  半凝結時倒在餅摸內。雪凍取出切
  片。

Ingredients:

4 oz (112 g) sago
3 cups boiling water
2 big mangoes
¾ oz (21 g) agar agar
5½ cups water
8 oz (224 g) sugar
1 cup milk
3 eggs

Method:

* *Simmer the sago in the boiling water till transparent. Refresh and drain.*
* *Peel and dice the mangoes for later use.*
* *Soak the agar agar in some water for 1 hour then wash and towel dry. Pour the water in a saucepan and bring to the boil. Add the agar agar and sugar to simmer until both are dissolved.*
* *Turn off the heat and stir in the milk to mix well.*
* *Beat the eggs to mix with the sago and mangoes. Blend into the syrup and sit on a basin of crushed ice to whisk until half-set. Pour into the jelly mould to chill in the refrigerator.*

月 餅 糖 膠
Moon Cake Syrup

材料：

粗砂糖21安（588克）
棉白糖 6 安（168克）
† 舊糖漿 ¾ 杯
清水 3 杯
檸檬 1 個

製法：

* 粗砂糖、棉白糖、舊糖漿及清水一同放在鍋內以中火煮沸。加入檸檬汁後轉用慢火熬約 1 小時，煮至糖漿滴在水中不散開而起軟珠即可。如糖膠太硬時，可加水再煮片刻。

結果：

約 2 磅（ 1 公斤）

† 如無舊糖漿。則新製糖膠必須放置數週後始可取用。

Ingredients:

21 oz (588 g) crystal sugar
6 oz (168 g) icing sugar
³/₄ cup old syrup
3 cups water
1 lemon

Method:

* *Place the crystal sugar, icing sugar, old syrup and water in a saucepan to boil over medium heat. Drop in the lemon juice and lower the heat. Continue to simmer for about 1 hour. Test the syrup by putting a drop of it in the cold water. It should be soft and pliable when cooled. If it is too hard, add some water to simmer again. Yields about 2 lbs (1 kg). This syrup is best used after 3 months.*

月 餅 皮
Moon Cake Pastry

材料：

麵粉10安（280克）
糖漿¾杯
生油½杯
梘水½茶匙

製法：

* 麵粉篩在桌上開穴，將糖漿、生油、梘水放入穴中拌勻。慢慢將四週麵粉撥入搓成一軟糰。放置3小時後方能取用。否則月餅不容易敲出。

* 將軟糰搓成長條，切成每糰1¼安（35克）等份。

* 將每等份放在桌上，以手掌按成中央略厚，週圍略薄之圓形，將餡料放在中央包住，放入已洒粉之餅模中按平。將模向左右邊一敲，再向中央一敲即將餅敲落在手中，排放已塗油之餅盤中，預備入爐。

Ingredients:

10 oz (280 g) plain flour
³/4 cup syrup
¹/2 cup oil
¹/2 tsp alkali water

Method:

* *Sift 8 oz (224 g) of the flour on to a table and make a well in the centre. Put in the syrup, oil and alkali water to mix thoroughly.*
* *Gradually draw in the flour to knead into a soft dough and put aside for ¹/2 hour. Sprinkle in the remaining flour and leave aside for 2¹/2 hours to avoid from sticking to the mould.*
* *Knead the dough into a long roll. Cut into 1¹/4 oz (35 g) equal portions to wrap in the filling.*
* *Dust the cake mould with a little flour. Press the dough into the mould and knock it out. Arrange on to a greased baking tray and get ready to bake in the oven.*

69

月蓮椰黄蛋
Moon Cake with Coconut

材料：

冰肉 1 ½ 安（42克）
糕粉 2 安（56克）
棉糖 4 安（112克）
糖蓮子 3 安（84克）
欖仁 1 安（28克）
椰茸 4 安（112克）
水 2 湯匙
豬油 2 湯匙
油 1 湯匙
熟鹹蛋黃 4 隻
另糕粉 1 茶匙
月餅皮 6 安（168克）
蛋黃 1 隻塗面

製法：

* 冰肉切成幼粒。以上述少許羔粉撈勻。加入棉白糖混和置桌上開穴。
* 將糖蓮子、杭仁、椰蓉、水及豬油全部放入和勻，最後加入羔粉及生油搓成一軟糰。
* 咸蛋黃用另一茶匙羔粉洒勻。
* 將餡料分作 4 份，每份中央放一咸蛋黃約 5½ 安（154克）重，以餅皮包裹。置洒粉餅模中按實後敲出，排放在塗油焗盆上。
* 以噴水壺噴水在餅上後，放入400度（煤氣6度）焗爐內焗約 5 分鐘，取出薄薄塗上一層蛋液，將餅盤掉轉後，減低爐火至 300度（煤氣2度）再焗15至18分鐘，取出攤凍即成。

Ingredients:

1¹/2 oz (42 g) candied pork
2 oz (56 g) cooked glutinous rice flour
4 oz (112 g) icing sugar
3 oz (84 g) candied lotus seeds
1 oz (28 g) olive kernels
4 oz (112 g) desiccated coconut
2 tbsp water
2 tbsp lard
1 tbsp oil
4 cooked salted egg yolks
1 extra tsp cooked glutinous rice flour
6 oz (168 g) moon cake dough
1 beaten egg yolk

Method:

* *Dice and mix the candied pork with one quarter of the cooked glutinous rice flour. Add the icing sugar to mix thoroughly. Place on to the table to make a well in the centre.*
* *Put in the candied lotus seeds, olive kernels, desiccated coconut, water and lard to mix evenly. Sprinkle in the remaining cooked glutinous rice flour and oil to knead into a soft dough.*
* *Coat the salted egg yolks with the extra tsp of cooked glutinous rice flour.*
* *Divide the filling into 4 portions to wrap in 1 egg yolk. Weighing 5¹/2 oz (154 g) each. Divide the dough into 4 portions and press into 4 rounds. Place the filling on the flattened dough to wrap up neatly. Press into a floured cake mould. Knock the cake out to put on a greased baking tray.*
* *Spray some water on the moon cakes then put into a preheated 400°F (Gas Mark 6) oven to bake for 5 minutes. Brush each cake with a thin layer of the beaten egg yolk. Return the tray into the oven. Reduce the heat to 300°F (Gas Mark 2) to bake for another 15 to 18 minutes. Remove and leave to cool.*

豆 蓉 餡

Mung Bean Paste for Moon Cake

材料：

油 1⅓杯
葱 3 條或葱頭 3 粒
水 2 — 3 杯
黃水數滴
鹽 3 茶匙
糖 2 磅（1 公斤）
綠豆粉 1¼ 磅（560克）

製法：

* 燒紅鑊，將油倒入煮沸炸香青葱棄
  去，停火把油略攤凍。
* 水 3 杯放大碗中，加黃水及鹽和勻
  後倒在油中和勻。
* 將糖加入以中火煮沸至糖完全溶化
  即可停火。將粉加入搞勻後。再以
  中火不停撹動至杰身即成。

結果：

約 2½磅

Ingredients:

1¹/₃ cups oil
3 chives or shallots
2 cups water
¹/₄ tsp yellow food colouring
3 tsp salt
2 lb (1 kg) sugar
20 oz (560 g) mung bean powder

Method:

* *Heat the wok to bring the oil to the boil. Saute the chives and discard. Turn off the heat and leave to cool for a while.*
* *Drop the yellow colouring and salt in the water until evenly dispersed then pour into the oil to stir well.*
* *Add the sugar to boil over moderate heat until dissolved. Turn off the heat then sift in the mung bean powder and stir continuously until a thick paste is formed. Yields about 2¹/₂ lbs (1¹/₄ kg).*

红豆沙餡

Sweet Red Bean Paste for Moon Cake

材料：

紅豆20安（560克）
水 5 杯
糖 1½ 磅（672克）
油 1⅔ 杯

製法：

* 紅豆洗淨，加水同放壓力保中煮沸
  。轉用中火續煮30分鐘。倒在疏篩
  內以売力搓。將豆沙壓出篩外，落
  在桶中。
* 將豆沙倒在燒熱之鑊中。以鑊鏟搓
  至略乾身。即將糖傾入煮沸，加油
  同搓至杰身即可。

Ingredients:

20 oz (560 g) red beans
5 cups water
1¹/₂ lb (³/₄ kg) sugar
1²/₃ cups oil

Method:

* *Wash and drain the red beans.*
* *Bring the water and red beans to boil in a pressure cooker. Continue to boil over moderate heat for 30 minutes. Pour into a strainer and press the red beans through to form a smooth purée.*
* *Put the red bean purée in a heated wok and stir continously over low heat until dry. Add the sugar and oil to mix into a thick paste. Remove and leave to cool. Yields 3¹/₂ lbs.*

牛脷酥
Ox Tongue Crisp

材料：

皮——麵種 4 安（112克）
　　　糖 2½ 安（70克）
　　　梳打粉 ⅜ 茶匙
　　　臭粉 ⅜ 茶匙
　　　水 ¾ 杯
　　　筋粉 8 安（224克）
　　　麵粉 2 安（56克）

酥心—豬油 1 湯匙
　　　臭粉 ⅛ 茶匙
　　　糖 1 安（28克）
　　　水 1 湯匙
　　　麵粉 3 安（84克）

製法：

皮—
* 麵種、糖、梳打粉及臭粉同放大盆中，慢慢注入水和勻成糊。
* 筋粉、麵粉同篩在桌上開穴，將粉糊倒在中央，輕輕撥入四週粉料按成軟糰。以毛巾蓋住發 3 小時。

酥心—
* 豬油與臭粉同撈勻。糖加入水中拌溶。一同放入大盆中，篩入麵粉再搓成一軟糰。雪凍候用。

完成—
* 取出皮料輾成 8½吋×12吋（21×30公分）長方形。酥心亦輾成 4 吋×12吋（10×30公分）窄長方，舖在皮之一邊。另一邊留½吋（1.2公分）收口，以手指捏緊。蓋住再發 1 小時。
* 將發妥麵糰切成 ¾吋×4 吋（2×10公分）長條，兩頭捏尖，滑入熱油鑊中炸至金黃色，撈起隔去油。

Ingredients:

Outer Dough-
4 oz (112 g) yeast dough
2¹/₂ oz (70 g) sugar

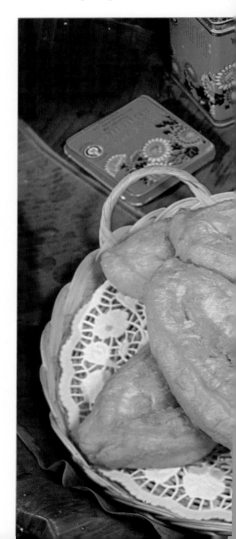

2/3 tsp soda bicarbonate
2/3 tsp ammonia soda
3/4 cup water
8 oz (224 g) high protein flour
2 oz (56 g) plain flour

Filling-
1 tbsp lard
1/6 tsp ammonia soda
1 oz (28 g) sugar
1 tbsp water
3 oz (84 g) flour
1/2 wok hot oil

Method:

Outer Dough-
* Place the yeast dough, sugar soda and ammonia in a mixing bowl. Gradually pour in the water to mix evenly until a paste is formed.
* Sift the high protein and plain flour on to the table. Make a well in the centre and put in the yeast dough paste. Draw in the flour and knead into a smooth dough. Cover with a damp cloth and leave to prove for 3 hours.

Filling-
* Mix the lard with the ammonia then dissolve the sugar in the water. Place all these in a mixing bowl. Sift in the flour and mix until smooth. Chill in the refrigerator for later use.

To Complete-
* Roll the outer dough into a rectangular sheet of 8½" x 12" (21 x 30 cm) then egg-wash the surface. Shape the filling into an oblong of 4" x 12" (10 x 30 cm) and place lengthwise on top, leaving ½" (1.2 cm) away from the edge on one side. Fold the dough to enclose the filling within. Seal securely along the ½" (1.2 cm) edge. Cover with a damp towel and leave aside to prove for another hour.
* Cut the dough crosswise into strips of ¾" x 4" (2 x 10 cm). Using the thumb and forefinger, pinch both ends of the strip to form two sharp points. Slip in the hot oil to deep fry until golden brown. Drain and serve hot or cold.

牛肉鍋貼
Pan Stickers with Minced Beef

材料：

皮－ 麵粉10安（280克）
　　凍水⅓杯
　　沸水½杯
　　鹽少許
餡－ 牛肉10安（280克）
　　馬蹄 5 隻
　　榨菜1安（28克）

製法：

皮－
* 麵粉篩過，分成二等份。一份用凍水搓勻，另一份則用沸水搓勻。然後兩份加鹽同搓成軟糰，用毛巾蓋著。

餡－
* 牛肉攪爛，用生抽2茶匙，糖1茶匙，梳打粉¼茶匙，生粉1茶匙，胡椒粉少許，水½杯，油2湯匙和勻醃30分鐘。加入剁碎馬蹄及榨菜一同拌勻。

完成－
* 麵糰取出搓成一長條，切成24等份。每一份以木棍輾成圓形。放入2茶匙餡料後收邊。
* 煎鍋燒紅，塗油少許。將鍋貼排在鍋中煮2分鐘。加水½杯。蓋上鑊蓋，以文火煮5分鐘。揭蓋再加油少許續煎3分鐘，至底部呈金黃色即成。將鍋貼倒轉上碟。

Ingredients:

Pastry-
10 oz (280 g) plain flour
¹/₃ cup cold water
¹/₂ cup boiling water
¹/₂ tsp salt

Filling-
10 oz (280 g) beef
5 water chestnuts
1 oz (28 g) pickled mustard

Seasoning-
1 tbsp oil
¹/₂ cup salted water
1 tsp sesame oil

Method:

Pastry-
* *Sift the flour then divide into 2 equal portions. Knead one portion with the cold water and the other with the boiling water and salt. Combine to knead into a soft dough. Cover with a damp towel.*

Filling-
* *Mince the beef and marinate with 2 tsp soy, 1 tsp each of cornflour and sugar, ¹/₂ tsp wine, ¹/₈ tsp pepper, ¹/₂ cup water and 2 tbsp oil for 30 minutes. Add the minced water chestnuts and pickled mustard to mix well.*

To Complete-
* *Remove the dough to knead into a long roll. Cut into 24 equal portions. Roll each piece into thin rounds to place in 2 tsp of filling. Draw the edges together to seal neatly.*
* *Heat the pan till very hot then grease with some oil. Arrange the pan stickers into the pan to cook for 2 minutes. Add the salted water then cover to simmer over low heat for 5 minutes. Remove the lid to add the sesame oil. Continue to cook for a further 3 minutes. Place the pan stickers up side down on a dish and serve.*

九 江 煎 堆
Popcorn Cakes in Batter
(Kow Kong Gin Dwei)

材料：

皮一麵粉20安（560克）
　　發粉 3 茶匙
　　包種 5 安（140克）
　　溫水 2 杯
　　沙糖 4 安（112克）
　　豬油 3 湯匙

餡一花生 6 安（168克）
　　炮谷20安（560克）
　　片糖10安（280克）
　　水 1 杯
　　芝蔴 1 安（28克）

製法：

皮一
* 麵粉、發粉同篩在盆中開穴。
* 包種放溫水中搓溶，加在麵粉穴中
  拌勻成濃漿。放置溫暖地方發 5 小
  時。
* 將沙糖及溶豬油加入和勻。

餡一
* 花生以水略浸後滴乾，放焗爐中焗
  脆。去衣剁碎，與炮谷同放大盆中
  。
* 片糖加水煮成糖膠，傾在炮谷中拌
  勻。
* 芝蔴洗淨，以白鑊烙乾，炒至黃色
  即加入炮谷中和勻，以手按實成大
  餅。
* 將每個大餅放在粉漿內沾勻，隨即
  放入沸油中炸至金黃色浮起。

Ingredients:

Pastry-
20 oz (560 g) flour
3 tsp baking powder
5 oz (140 g) yeast dough
2 cups warm water
4 oz (112 g) fine sugar
3 tbsp lard

Filling-
6 oz (168 g) peanuts
20 oz (560 g) popcorn
10 oz (280 g) brown sugar
1 cup water
1 oz (28 g) sesame seeds

¹/₂ wok boiling oil

Method:

Pastry-
* *Sift the flour and baking powder
  in a bowl then make a well in the
  centre.*
* *Dissolve the yeast dough in the
  warm water then pour into the
  centre of the bowl to mix into a
  thick batter. Leave aside
  to prove in a warm place for 4 to 5
  hours.*
* *Add the sugar and melted lard to
  mix thoroughly.*

Filling-
* *Soak the peanuts in the water
  until double the size. Drain and
  bake in the oven until crisp. Peel
  and crush. Put in the bowl to
  mix with the popcorn.*
* *Simmer the brown sugar with
  the water to form a syrup and
  pour over the popcorn.*
* *Wash and parch the sesame
  seeds until golden then mix with
  the popcorn. Using the hands,
  press into big round cakes.*
* *Dip each cake into the batter to
  coat evenly. Deep fry in the boiling oil until golden brown.
  Remove and drain on absorbent
  paper.*

西米水晶餅

Sago Crystal Cakes

材料：

西米 7 安（196克）
糖 2 安（56克）
奶水 3 湯匙
汀麵 4 安（112克）
豬油 1 湯匙
蓮蓉12安（336克）

製法：

* 西米用清水浸30分鐘。
* 鍋中放水½鍋，煮沸後將西米倒入煮片刻。熄火焗 1 小時至透明。放水喉下沖凍及洗去膠質，隔清水份。
* 將糖及奶水放在大盆中混和，篩入汀麵搞勻，即將西米倒入拌成漿狀。置塗油碟中蒸10分鐘。取出加豬油搓成軟糰。
* 蓮蓉分成需要之等份。
* 將軟粉糰搓成長條，切成等份，以手壓扁放入蓮蓉一份。收口將粉糰放入塗油餅模中壓實，用力將餅敲出。
* 將餅排放在塗油蒸籠內蒸 8 分鐘，即可取出。

Ingredients:

7 oz (l96 g) sago
2 oz (56 g) sugar
3 tbsp milk
4 oz (112 g) wheat starch
1 tbsp lard
12 oz (336 g) lotus seed paste

Method:

* Soak the sago for 30 minutes.
* Gently bring $^1/_2$ saucepan of water to boil and add the sago to cook for a while. Leave to soak for 1 hour till transparent. Remove and wash under a running tap and drain.
* Put the sugar and milk into a mixing bowl then sift in the wheat starch to stir well. Add the sago to mix into a soft paste. Place into a greased platter to steam for 10 minutes. Add the lard to knead into a soft dough.
* Divide the lotus seed paste into equal portions.
* Knead the dough into a cylinder and cut into equal portions. Press into a nest and place in a portion of paste. Draw the edges to seal. Press tightly into a greased cake mould and knock it out.
* Arrange into a greased steamer to cook for 8 minutes. Serve hot.

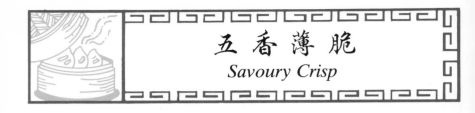

五香薄脆
Savoury Crisp

材料：

筋粉10安（280克）
發粉 $\frac{1}{2}$ 茶匙
梳打粉 $\frac{1}{4}$ 茶匙
五香粉 1 茶匙
南乳汁 2 湯匙
水 $\frac{1}{3}$ 杯
雞蛋 2 隻
糖 1 茶匙
黑芝蔴 1 湯匙

製法：

* 將筋粉及全部乾成份篩在桌上開穴。
* 南乳汁與水和勻，再與蛋，糖及芝蔴一同放穴中拌溶。將四週之粉撥入搓成軟糰。
* 桌上篩粉少許將麵糰分爲12塊，輾薄切成長方薄片。
* 將薄片切成小長條再剪成小三角。置沸油中炸至金黃色，撈起攤凍。

Ingredients:

10 oz (280 g) high protein floour
$^1/_2$ tsp baking powder
$^1/_4$ tsp soda bicarbonate
1 tsp spicy powder
2 tbsp fermented bean curd sauce
$^1/_3$ cup water
2 eggs
1 tsp sugar
1 tbsp black sesame seeds
$^1/_2$ wok oil

Method:

* *Sift the flour, baking powder, soda and spicy powder on to the table and make a well in the centre.*
* *Mix the fermented bean curd sauce with the water. Pour the mixture into the well with the shelled eggs, sugar and sesame seeds to mix thoroughly. Draw in the flour to knead into a soft dough.*
* *Dust the table with some flour then divide the dough into 12 equal portions. Roll each portion into paper-thin oblong piece. Cut into small triangles or any other shapes.*
* *Bring the oil to boil over medium heat then deep fry the triangles till golden.*

鮮荷葉飯
Savoury Rice in Lotus Leaf

材料：

熟冬菇 4 隻
草菰 2 安（56克）
叉燒 3 安（84克）
燒鴨 3 安（84克）
蝦仁 3 安（84克）
蛋 1 隻
白飯 3 杯
鮮蓮葉 1 張

調味一生抽 1 湯匙
　　　糖 1 茶匙
　　　胡椒粉少許
　　　蔴油½ 茶匙

製法：

* 冬菇切粒留用。
* 草菰去蒂飛水切粒。
* 叉燒、燒鴨亦切粒。
* 蝦挑腸洗淨抹乾，以胡椒粉、生粉略撈後泡油撈起候用。
* 蛋打爛煎成蛋皮切粒。
* 燒紅鑊，加油 1 湯匙煮沸。將冬菇、草菰及所有粒料倒入略兜，加入少許調味隨即收火將飯及調味料倒入和勻。
* 荷葉以沸水拖過抹乾，塗以豬油。將飯倒入包好，用草略紮。放蒸籠內大火蒸30分鐘。取出剪開荷葉即可進食。

Ingredients:

4 cooked mushrooms
2 oz (56 g) straw mushrooms
3 oz (84 g) roast pork
3 oz (84 g) roast duck
3 oz (84 g) shelled shrimps
$1/8$ tsp pepper
$1/2$ tsp cornflour
1 egg
$1^1/2$ tbsp oil
3 cups cooked rice
1 large lotus leaf

Seasoning-
1 tbsp light soy
1 tsp sugar
$1/8$ tsp pepper
1 tsp sesame oil

Method:

* *Dice the cooked mushrooms. Trim, blanch, refresh and dice the straw mushrooms.*
* *Dice the roast pork and duck.*
* *Devein, clean and dry the shrimps with a towel. Coat with the pepper and cornflour then parboil in the warm oil and drain for later use.*
* *Beat the egg and shallow fry with $1/2$ tbsp of oil to make an egg sheet then dice.*
* *Reheat the wok to bring the remaining oil to boil. Saute the diced ingredients for a while. Add the seasoning and turn off the heat. Stir in the rice to mix evenly.*
* *Blanch, rinse and dry the lotus leaf. Grease with some lard and pour in the mixed rice to fold up neatly. Tie with a straw and steam for 30 minutes. Remove and serve hot.*

五 香 煎 堆
Savoury Sesame Balls

材料：

皮一薯仔12安（336克）
　　水 1/2 杯
　　糖 2 安（56克）
　　糯米粉 8 安（224克）
　　芝蔴 1/2 杯
餡一瘦肉 4 安（112克）
　　熟冬菇 4 隻
　　蝦米 1 安（28克）
　　馬蹄 2 安（56克）
　　葱頭茸 1/2 茶匙
　　葱粒 1 湯匙

調味一酒 1/2 茶匙
　　　水 2 湯匙
　　　糖 1 茶匙
　　　五香粉 1 茶匙
　　　蠔油 1 茶匙
　　　蔴油 1/4 茶匙
　　　生粉水 1 茶匙

製法：

皮一
* 薯仔焓熟去皮搓爛成茸。
* 水放在另一個煲中加糖煮溶。
* 糯米粉篩在深盆中開穴，將糖水沖入穴中與粉和勻。再將薯茸加入糯米粉糰搓成軟糰。以毛巾蓋着候用。

餡一
* 瘦肉切粒，用生抽 1 茶匙、糖酒各 1/2 茶匙和勻醃10分鐘，泡油候用。
* 冬菇切粒、蝦米浸透切粒、馬蹄去皮亦切粒。
* 燒紅鑊，加油 1 湯匙爆香葱頭茸。倒下蝦米爆透，隨將全部材料傾入炒勻，調妥味以生粉水埋饋上碟攤凍。

完成一
* 粉糰搓成長條，分切32等份。以手按扁，放入一份餡料捏緊成圓球形。置芝蔴上打滾後，再放熱油中炸至金黃色，撈起隔油。

Ingredients:

Pastry-
12 oz (336 g) potatoes
1/2 cup water
2 oz (56 g) sugar
8 oz (224 g) glutinous rice flour
1/2 cup sesame seeds

Filling-
4 oz (112 g) pork loin
4 cooked mushrooms
1 oz (28 g) dried shrimps
2 oz (56 g) water chestnuts
1/2 tsp mashed shallot

1 tbsp chopped chives

Seasoning-
1/2 tsp wine
2 tbsp water
1 tsp sugar
1 tsp five spice powder
1 tsp oyster sauce
1/4 tsp sesame oil
1 tsp cornflour mix

Method:

Pastry-
* Clean and boil the potatoes till soft. Peel and mash into a pulp.
* Bring the water to boil in a small saucepan to dissolve the sugar.
* Sift the glutinous rice flour on to the table and make a well in the centre to put in the mashed potatoes and syrup. Gradually draw in the flour to knead into a soft dough. Cover with a towel and leave for later use.

Filling-
* Dice the pork and marinate with 1 tsp soy, 1/2 tsp sugar and wine for 10 minutes. Parboil in 2 cups of oil and drain, leaving 1 tbsp oil for sautéeing.
* Dice the mushrooms. Soak and dice the dried shrimps. Peel and dice the water chestnuts.
* Heat the wok with oil to sauté the shallot and dried shrimps. Stir in the other ingredients to mix well. Sizzle the wine and season to taste. Thicken the sauce with the cornflour mix. Dish and leave to cool.

To Complete-
* Roll the dough into a cylinder and divide into 32 equal portions. Press each into a flat round and place in 1 tsp of filling. Draw in the edges to seal into balls. Coat with the sesame seeds and deep fry till golden brown. Remove and drain.

笑 口 常 開
Sesame Cookies

材料：

清水 4 湯匙
幼糖 5 安（140克）
雞蛋 1 隻
油 2 湯匙
白麵粉10安（280克）
發粉 ½ 茶匙
梳打粉 ½ 茶匙
芝麻 ½ 杯

製法：

* 清水放鍋內煮沸加糖搞溶。
* 雞蛋與油同放碗中和勻候用。
* 麵粉、發粉、梳打粉一同篩在桌上
  開穴。將糖水及蛋、油放入拌勻，
  慢慢把四週麵粉撥入以手按妥。搓
  成長條，分切成32等份。
* 芝麻預先洗淨隔乾水份，放圓兜或
  大碗中。將切成等份之小麵糰搓圓
  ，放入滾上一層芝麻。
* 油大半鍋煮至大熱時，熄火將圓球
  放入炸至發大裂開。重開中火炸至
  金黃色，以罩籬撈起隔淨餘油。攤
  凍後置瓶中可留一個月。

Ingredients:

4 tbsp water
5 oz (140 g) sugar
1 egg
2 tbsp oil
10 oz (280 g) plain flour
½ tsp baking powder
½ tsp soda bicarbonate
½ cup sesame seeds
½ wok oil

Method:

* *Bring the water to boil in a small
  saucepan. Turn off the heat to
  stir in the sugar till dissolves.*
* *Beat the egg with the oil.*
* *Sift the flour, baking powder
  and soda on to the table. Make a
  well in the centre to put in the
  syrup and egg batter. Slowly
  draw in the flour to form a soft
  dough. Divide into 32 equal portions and shape into small balls.*
* *Wash, drain and dry the sesame
  seeds. Roll the small balls on the
  seeds to coat evenly.*
* *Bring the oil to just boil then slip
  in the cookies to deep fry over
  low heat till a crack is formed.
  Increase the heat to deep fry till
  golden brown. Remove and
  drain on absorbent paper. Leave
  to cool then store in a jar.*

芝麻餅仔
Sesame Crisps

材料：

麵粉10安（280克）
梳打粉½茶匙
豬油3½湯匙（98克）
水⅓杯
糖4安（112克）
雞蛋1隻
芝蔴1杯

製法：

* 麵粉蒸熟（約10分鐘），以木棍滾開篩勻開穴。
* 放入梳打、豬油。
* 糖加水煮溶立刻倒入穴內拌勻。
* 攤凍輾成½吋薄片，以花級級成圓形。
* 將小圓餅兩邊塗上雞蛋，放芝蔴中沾滿餅面。焗爐開定300度（煤氣2度），放中格焗10至15分鐘至金黃色。

Ingredients:

10 oz (280 g) flour
¹/₂ tsp soda bicarbonate
3¹/₂ tbsp lard
¹/₃ cup water
4 oz (112 g) sugar
1 beaten egg
1 cup sesame seeds

Method:

* *Place the flour in a steamer to cook for 10 minutes. Remove and break the lumps with a rolling pin. Sift on to the table and make a well in the centre.*
* *Place the soda and lard into the well.*
* *Bring the water to boil in a saucepan to dissolve the sugar. Pour the syrup into the well to mix with the soda and lard. Draw in the flour to knead into a soft dough.*
* *Roll the dough into a ¹/₈ inch (3 mm) sheet then cut into small rounds with a cutter.*
* *Brush both sides of the biscuits with the beaten egg and coat with the sesame seeds. Bake in a preheated 300°F (Gas Mark 2) oven for 10 to 15 minutes until golden. Remove and serve.*

蕉葉軟糍

Snow Balls in Banana Leaves

材料：

皮—糯米粉 8 安（224克）
　　粘米粉 2 安（56克）
　　沸水 1 杯
　　豬油¾安（21克）

餡—花生½杯
　　芝蔴 2 湯匙
　　椰茸¼杯
　　糖¾杯

製法：

皮—
*　糯米粉與粘米粉同篩在大盆中，迅
　速倒入沸水用木棍搞勻成一軟糰。
　加入豬油再搓勻。用毛巾蓋著放置
　一旁。

餡—
*　花生浸於沸水內約20分鐘。置中火
　焗爐中焗脆，取出剁碎。
*　芝蔴洗淨，隔乾水份後以白鑊烙乾。
*　花生茸、芝蔴、椰茸及糖放在盆中
　拌勻。

完成—
*　將粉糰分成24等份。用手掌壓成扁
　圓形。放入1至2茶匙餡料，以手捏
　邊收口，每個軟糍底部放一小塊塗
　油蕉葉。置蒸籠內蒸 5 分鐘。

Ingredients:

Pastry-
8 oz (224 g) glutinous rice flour
2 oz (56 g) rice flour
1 cup boiling water
³/₄ oz (21 g) lard

Filling-
¹/₂ cup peanuts
1 cup boiling water
2 tbsp sesame seeds
¹/₄ cup desiccated coconut
³/₄ cup sugar

Method:

Pastry-
* Sift both the flour into a mixing
  bowl and pour in the boiling
  water to stir quickly with a
  wooden spoon till a soft dough is
  formed. Add the lard to knead
  evenly. Cover with a damp towel
  and leave aside.

Filling-
* Soak the peanuts in the boiling
  water for 20 minutes then toast
  in the preheated 250°F (Gas
  Mark ¹/₂) oven till crisp.
  Remove and chop finely.
* Wash, drain and parch the
  sesame seeds.
* Place the chopped peanuts,
  sesame seeds, coconut and sugar
  in a bowl to mix thoroughly.

To Complete-
* Cut the dough into 24 equal portions. Press each into a round
  flat piece and fill each round
  with 2 tsp of the filling. Draw the
  edges together to seal tightly.
  Arrange each ball on a piece of
  greased oval shaped banana
  leaf. Fold and seal the leaf with a
  toothpick. Cook in a steamer for
  5 minutes then remove.

五香蠶豆
Spicy Broad Beans

材料：

蠶豆 1 磅（½ 公斤）
水 5 杯
八角 3 粒
鹽 2 至 3 茶匙
糖 1 茶匙

製法：

* 蠶豆以水預早一天浸至發漲。
* 鍋中放水，將豆傾入再加八角、鹽及糖一同煮沸。文火續燜 1 小時至豆軟。
* 停火將豆倒出，隔乾水份即可食用。

Ingredients:

1 lb (¹/₂ kg) broad beans
5 cups water
3 star anises
2 tsp salt
1 tsp sugar

Method:

* *Soak the broad beans for 24 hours until the beans are double in size.*
* *Fill a saucepan with the water and put in the broad beans. Add the star anises, salt and sugar to bring to the boil. Simmer for 1 hour till the broad beans are soft and tender.*
* *Remove and drain. Leave to cool then serve as snack.*

鹹 煎 餅
Spicy Doughnuts

材料：

皮—麵種10安（280克）
　　幼糖7安（196克）
　　水 1 杯
　　梳打粉½安（14克）
　　鹼水¼茶匙
　　高筋粉 1¼磅（560克）

餡—南乳 2 湯匙
　　五香粉 1 茶匙
　　鹽 1 茶匙

製法：

* 麵種、糖及水同放盆中，以手搞勻
  至糖溶。
* 加入梳打粉及鹼水，篩入麵粉一同
  拌挼，搓成一麵糰。
* 用拳頭輕壓麵糰使軟滑，對摺再壓
  。將麵糰以雙拳壓平向內摺成三幅
  。再以拳輕按10分鐘。置一旁約半
  小時。
* 取出再以拳按 5 分鐘後用半濕毛巾
  蓋著；放置 1 小時待發。
* 將麵糰以木棍輾成½吋厚，10吋闊
  之長條；餡料和勻，薄薄舖在上面
  ，然後向外捲起，放置一旁再發一
  小時。將麵卷切成約一吋厚之圓餅
  ，以手略按扁。
* 將每個圓餅放入熱油內炸至浮起。
  不時反轉至定型及金黃色即可撈起
  。

Ingredients:

Pastry-
10 oz (280 g) yeast dough
7 oz (196 g) sugar
1 cup water
¹/₂ oz (14 g) soda bicarbonate
¹/₄ tsp alkali water
1¹/₄ lb (560 g) high protein flour

Filling-
2 tbsp fermented red bean curd
1 tsp five spice powder
1 tsp salt

Method:

* *Place the yeast dough, sugar and water in a bowl to mix thoroughly by hand till the sugar dissolves.*
* *Drop in the soda and alkali water. Sift in the flour to bind well.*
* *Use the fists to press the dough and make it smooth. Fold the dough together and press again. Flatten the dough with both fists to fold into one-third and press again. Repeat for 10 minutes. Leave aside for 30 minutes.*
* *Press again for 5 minutes and cover with a damp cloth. Leave aside for 1 hour.*
* *Roll the pastry into a rectangular sheet about ¹/₂" (1.2 cm) thick and 10" (25 cm) wide. Spread the filling on the sheet and roll up. Leave aside to prove for at least 1 hour before deep frying.*
* *Cut into 1" (2.5 cm) thick portions and flatten into round thin pieces.*
* *Slide into the hot oil to deep fry over moderate heat. When the doughnuts begin to float, turn continously until the shape is formed. Deep fry till golden brown then remove and drain.*

鷄 球 大 飽
Steamed Buns with Chicken

材料：

皮一麵種 1½ 磅（672克）
　　沙糖 6 安（168克）
　　鹼水 ¾ 茶匙
　　豬油 2 湯匙
　　臭粉 1 茶匙
　　水 1 湯匙
　　麵粉 8 安（224克）
　　發粉 2 茶匙

餡一雞肉 6 安（168克）
　　燒腩 6 安（168克）
　　咸蛋 4 隻
　　熟冬菇 8 隻
　　紅蘿蔔 2 安（56克）
　　葱 3 棵

調味一酒 1 茶匙
　　　上湯 ¼ 杯
　　　蠔油 1 茶匙
　　　糖 ½ 茶匙
　　　生粉水 1 茶匙

製法：

皮一
* 將麵種倒入大盆中，加入糖、鹼水、豬油、臭粉及水拌勻，搓成漿狀。
* 麵粉、發粉篩在桌上開穴，將麵種糊倒在穴中。撥入四週麵粉搓成一軟糰。以布蓋着置一旁候用。

餡一
* 雞肉切16件，以羌汁、酒、生抽、生粉各 1 茶匙、糖½ 茶匙、胡椒粉少許和勻醃15分鐘。泡油候用。
* 燒腩切16件。咸蛋焓熟去殼，每只分切四件。冬菇開邊。紅蘿蔔切絲。葱切粒。
* 燒紅鑊加油煮沸，灒酒傾入上湯，調妥味以生粉水埋艬，熄火將各物倒入拌勻。盛起攤凍。

完成一
* 將麵糰放在洒粉之案板上，分切16份。以手捏成窩形，將一份餡料放入打摺埋口，以白紙墊底，置蒸籠內猛火蒸10分鐘即成。

Ingredients:

Pastry-
1¹/₂ lb (672 g) yeast dough
6 oz (168 g) sugar
³/₄ tsp alkali water
2 tbsp lard
1 tsp ammonia soda
1 tbsp water
8 oz (224 g) plain flour
2 tsp baking powder

Filling-
6 oz (168 g) chicken meat
6 oz (168 g) roast belly pork
4 salted eggs
8 cooked mushrooms
2 oz (56 g) carrot
3 spring onions

Seasoning-
2 tbsp oil
1 tsp wine
¹/₄ cup stock

1 tsp oyster sauce
¹/₂ tsp sugar
1 tsp cornflour mix

Method:

Pastry-
* Put the yeast dough in a mixing bowl. Add the sugar, alkali water, lard, ammonia soda and the water to mix into a paste.
* Sift the flour and baking powder on to a table and make a well in the centre. Pour the yeast paste into the well. Draw in the flour to knead into a soft dough. Cover with a towel and leave aside for later use.

Filling-
* Cut the chicken meat into 16 pieces and marinate with 1 tsp each of ginger juice, wine, cornflour and soy, ³/₄ tsp sugar and ¹/₈ tsp pepper for 15 minutes. Parboil in the warm oil and drain.
* Cut the roast pork into 16 pieces. Poach the salted eggs then peel and quarter them. Halve each mushroom. Shred the carrot and dice the spring onions.
* Heat the wok and bring the oil to boil. Sizzle the wine and add the stock. Season and thicken the sauce with the cornflour mix. Remove from the heat and pour in all the ingredients to mix well. Leave aside to cool then divide into 16 portions.

To Complete-
* Place the dough on the floured table. Roll and divide into 16 portions then press each portion into a round. Put in a share of the filling and gather the edges to seal. With the sealed side facing up, stick a piece of white square paper underneath. Arrange in a steamer to cook for 10 minutes over high heat. Remove.

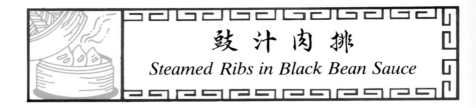

豉 汁 肉 排
Steamed Ribs in Black Bean Sauce

材料：

肉排 8 安（224克）
羌絲 1 茶匙
豆豉醬 2 茶匙
蒜頭 1 粒
葱 2 棵

調味一生抽 1 ½ 茶匙
　　　生粉 1 茶匙
　　　糖 1 茶匙
　　　酒 1 茶匙
　　　胡椒粉少許
　　　水 2 湯匙
　　　蔴油 1 茶匙

製法：

* 肉排洗淨斬成小件。加入羌絲、豆豉醬、剁爛蒜頭撈勻。
* 調味料同放小碗中，加水調勻倒在排骨上，再加油 1 湯匙混和。置蒸籠內之深碟中以中火蒸12分鐘。取出洒上葱絲。嗜辣者可加紅椒絲 1 湯匙。

Ingredients:

*8 oz (224 g) spare ribs
1 tsp shredded ginger
2 tsp fermented black bean paste
1 tsp minced garlic
2 shredded spring onions*

*Seasoning-
1½ tsp light soy
1 tsp cornflour
1 tsp sugar
1 tsp wine
⅛ tsp pepper
2 tbsp water
1 tsp sesame oil*

Method:

* *Wash and chop the ribs into small pieces. Stir in the shredded ginger, black bean paste and minced garlic to mix well.*
* *Place all the seasoning into a small bowl to stir till evenly mixed. Pour the mixed seasoning over the ribs and marinate for 30 minutes then blend in the sesame oil.*
* *Place the ribs on a platter and cook in a steamer over high heat for 12 minutes. Remove from the steamer and scatter the shredded spring onions on top. Serve hot.*

清 甜 豆 花

Sweet Bean Curd Jelly

材料：

大豆16安（½公斤）
清水26杯
熟石羔粉 3 茶匙
粟粉 1 安（28克）
另水½杯

製法：

* 大豆洗淨以水浸 6（夏天）至 10（冬天）小時。
* 將豆放水喉下再次沖洗。隔乾。
* 將豆分數次放在搞拌機內，加水共10杯磨成豆漿，以篩隔去豆渣，另用紗布再隔一次。
* 隔安之豆漿再加水至共成26杯。
* 將豆漿倒在鍋中文火煮沸至泡沫浮起三吋高。
* 石羔粉、粟粉同放小碗中加水½杯和勻。準備大盆一個將沸豆漿與石羔水同時傾入。以毛巾蓋住再覆以鍋蓋靜放15分鐘使凝結，放雪柜中雪凍。
* 食時以小碗盛起再加糖漿。

糖漿—

* 水 1 杯放鍋中加黃糖10安（280克）煮溶，每碗豆花約放糖漿2-3湯匙。

Ingredients:

1 lb (¹/₂ kg) soya beans
26 cups water
3 tsp plaster of Paris
1 oz (28 g) cornflour
extra ¹/₂ cup water

Light syrup-
1 cup water
10 oz (280 g) brown sugar

Method:

* *Wash the soya beans thoroughly then soak for 6 hours in summer and 10 hours during winter.*
* *Run the beans under cold water then drain.*
* *Using 10 cups of water, grind the beans into a liquid. Filter the liquid through a fine sieve first, then repeat the procedure by using a piece of muslin cloth.*
* *Add sufficient water to the liquid and make up to 26 cups of soya bean milk.*
* *Heat the bean milk to boiling point till it froths up.*
* *Dilute the plaster and cornflour in a bowl with the water. Pour the bean milk and the plaster mix rapidly into a large container. Cover with a towel and the lid. Leave aside for 15 minutes to set then chill in the refrigerator for 1 hour.*
* *Serve with the syrup.*

Light syrup-
* *Place the water and brown sugar in a saucepan. Leave to boil and simmer over low heat until the sugar dissolves. Serve each cup of soya bean jelly with 3 tbsp of syrup.*

豆沙酥餅
Sweet Red Bean Paste Patties

材料：

外皮－麵粉 6 安（168克）
　　　水 $\frac{1}{3}$ 杯
　　　油 2 湯匙
內皮－麵粉 4 安（112克）
　　　豬油 2$\frac{1}{2}$ 安（70克）
餡料－豆沙 12安（336克）
裝飾－蛋王 1 隻
　　　黑芝蔴 1 湯匙

製法：

外皮－
* 麵粉篩在桌上開穴，將水及油放在穴中拌勻。慢慢將四週麵粉撥入按成一軟糰。分成32等份。

內皮－
* 麵粉篩在桌上，加豬油搓成另一軟粉糰。

完成－
* 將內外兩粉糰各分成32等份。每份外皮按薄，放入一塊內皮後揑實。以木棍輾成一長條，向外捲起。重覆一次後即以木棍壓成小圓形。
* 將豆沙餡亦分成32等份。每份餡放在一個小圓皮上，打褶收口揑緊。收口處向下，以手按扁。
* 酥餅面塗上一層蛋黃液，洒上黑芝蔴。放入已預熱300度（煤氣2度）焗爐焗20分鐘，即可取出。

Ingredients:

Outer Pastry-
6 oz (168 g) plain flour
$^1/_3$ cup water
2 tbsp oil

Inner Pastry-
4 oz (112 g) plain flour
2$^1/_2$ oz (70 g) chilled lard

Filling-
12 oz (336 g) red bean paste

Decoration-
1 beaten egg yolk
1 tbsp black sesame seeds

Method:

Outer Pastry-
* *Sift the flour on to a table and make a well in the centre. Place the water and oil in the well to mix thoroughly. Slowly draw in the flour to knead into a smooth dough. Roll and cut into 32 equal portions.*

Inner Pastry-
* *Sift the flour on the table and mix with the lard to form another soft dough. Chill for 20 minutes then roll and cut into 32 equal portions.*

To Complete-
* *Press the outer pastry into a nest and put in a piece of inner pastry. Wrap up and press with a rolling pin. Flatten into a long strip and roll up like a jelly roll. Give the pastry a turn then roll up again. Repeat once then shape into a nest.*
* *Fill each nest with 1 portion of red bean paste. Draw the edges together to seal. Face the sealed edge downwards. Brush the beaten egg yolk on top and sprinkle with some sesame seeds.*
* *Bake in the preheated 300°F (Gas Mark 2) oven for 20 minutes.*

鴛鴦齋肚

Sweet Sour and Curry Gluten Balls

材料：

生筋球40個
葱頭 2 粒
蒜頭 2 粒
羌絲 2 茶匙

調味一1、 酒 1 茶匙
　　　　 酸甜醋⅔杯
　　　　 生抽 1 茶匙
　　　　 糖 1 茶匙
　　　　 味精¼茶匙
　　　　 胡椒粉少許
　　　　 生粉水 1 茶匙
　　 2、 咖喱醬 2 湯匙
　　　　 酒 1 茶匙
　　　　 上湯½杯
　　　　 生抽 1 茶匙
　　　　 糖 1 茶匙
　　　　 味精¼茶匙
　　　　 生粉水 1 茶匙

製法：

* 生筋球用沸水略拖後過冷水，隔乾
  水份分爲二份。
* 葱蒜頭切片後與羌絲同分爲二份。
* 燒紅鑊加油 2 湯匙煮沸爆香一份羌
  、葱、蒜。灒酒加酸甜醋及一份生
  筋球同煮約 3 分鐘，加入第一份調
  味料和勻續煮至水份將乾時，即可
  以生粉水打獻放在碟之一旁。
* 另鑊燒紅以油爆香另一份羌葱蒜，
  倒入咖喱醬及生筋球兜勻，灒酒加
  上湯及調味料煮片刻，以生粉水打
  獻排放在另一旁上桌。

Ingredients:

40 gluten balls
2 shallots
2 garlic cloves
2 tsp shredded ginger
2 tbsp oil

Seasoning-
1) 1 tsp wine
   ²/₃ cup sweet sour sauce
   1 tsp soy
   1 tsp sugar
   ¼ tsp chicken powder
   ⅛ tsp pepper
   1 tsp cornflour mix

2) 2 tbsp curry paste
   1 tsp wine
   ½ cup stock
   1 tsp soy
   1 tsp sugar
   ¼ tsp chicken powder
   1 tsp cornflour mix

Method:

* Blanch the gluten balls with some boiling water. Refresh and divide the balls into 2 portions.
* Crush the shallots and garlic. Divide into 2 portions.
* Heat the wok with half the oil to sauté half of the ginger, shallot and garlic. Sizzle the wine and pour in the sweet sour sauce. Slip in the first portion of gluten balls to simmer for 3 minutes. Season to taste with the first part of seasoning. Continue to simmer for 5 minutes. Thicken the sauce with the cornflour mix. Dish on one side of the platter.
* Heat another wok with the remaining oil to sauté the rest of the ginger, shallot, and garlic. Pour in the curry paste and the remaining gluten balls to mix well. Sizzle the wine and add the stock and seasoning. Thicken the gravy with the cornflour mix. Place on the other side of the platter then serve.

腐 皮 香 芋 卷
Taro Roll

材料：

腐皮 2 張
荔芋12安（336克）
豬肉 6 安（168克）
蝦米 1 安（28克）
葱 3 條
豬油 1 湯匙

調味一鹽½茶匙
　　　糖 2 茶匙
　　　酒 1 茶匙
　　　生抽 2 茶匙
　　　胡椒粉少許
　　　蔴油½茶匙
　　　生粉 1 湯匙

製法：

* 腐皮以濕布抹淨，以生粉水將 2 塊
　貼在一起，蓋住候用。
* 荔芋焓熟挾爛成芋茸。
* 豬肉洗淨剁成肉茸加入一半調味料
　撈勻醃15分鐘。
* 蝦米浸透剁爛，葱切粒。
* 將挾爛芋茸放在盆中，加入豬肉茸
　、蝦米、葱粒及其餘調味料和勻搞
　透。
* 腐皮攤開，將芋茸薄薄舖在上面向
　外捲成一長條，以生粉水收口，置
　塗油蒸籠內中火蒸12分鐘，取出攤
　凍切成棋子形，以繩略紮放入沸油
　中炸至金黃色，撈起隔去油，排入
　碟上。

Ingredients:

2 pieces bean curd sheet
3 tbsp cornflour mix
12 oz (336 g) taro or potatoes
6 oz (168 g) pork
1 oz (28 g) dried shrimps
3 spring onions
1 tbsp lard
½ wok hot oil

Seasoning-
½ tsp salt
2 tsp sugar
1 tsp wine
2 tsp light soy
⅛ tsp pepper
½ tsp sesame oil
1 tbsp cornflour
1 tbsp water

Method:

* Clean the bean curd sheets with a wet towel and paste the two sheets together with half of the cornflour mix. Cover with a damp cloth for later use.
* Steam the taro till cooked then mash.
* Wash and mince the pork. Marinate with half of the seasoning for 15 minutes.
* Soak the dried shrimps and mince finely. Chop the spring onions. Put the mashed taro into a mixing bowl then add the pork, dried shrimps, spring onions, lard and the remaining seasoning to mix till well blended.
* Spread the taro paste on the bean curd sheet and roll up into a cylinder of 2" (5 cm) diameter. Seal with the remaining of cornflour mix.
* Cook the taro roll in a greased steamer for 12 minutes. Remove and leave to cool. Cut into 1" (2.5 cm) thick rounds and tie each round with a piece of string to prevent the bean curd sheet from loosening.
* Deep fry in the hot oil till golden brown. Drain and dish.

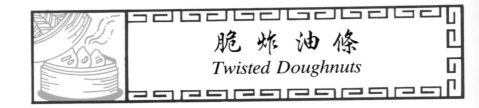

脆 炸 油 條
Twisted Doughnuts

材料：

筋粉20安（560克）
梳打粉 1 茶匙
鹽 2 茶匙
臭粉 ¾ 茶匙
水 1½ 杯

製法：

* 筋粉與梳打粉同篩在桌上開穴。將鹽、臭粉及水放入拌勻，慢慢將四週麵粉撥入和成一軟糰。
* 以雙拳將麵糰按約10分鐘，用毛巾蓋住。放置一旁發半小時。
* 取出再以雙拳按10分鐘至軟滑為止，以毛巾蓋住放置一旁再發 2 至 4 小時。
* 將麵糰用木棍輾成 3 吋長方條，約 ⅛ 吋厚。以刀切成 1 吋條子，每兩條疊起以刀背略按後，用手將條子拉長。
* 沸油 1 鍋將條子滑下以中火炸之，不停以罩籬略按及翻轉至發大定形時，再炸片刻至金黃色即撈起。

Ingredients:

20 oz (560 g) high protein flour
1 tsp soda bicarbonate
2 tsp salt
³/₄ tsp ammonia powder
1¹/₂ cups water
¹/₂ wok boiling oil

Method:

* *Sift the flour and soda on to the table. Make a well in the centre to put in the salt, ammonia powder and water. Mix well then work in the flour to form a smooth dough.*
* *Press the dough with both fists for 10 minutes. Cover with a towel and leave aside to prove for 30 minutes.*
* *Repeat the procedure for another 10 minutes or until it is smooth. Leave aside to prove for 4 hours.*
* *Roll the dough into a rectangular sheet, approximately 3" (7.5 cm) wide and ¹/₈" (3 mm) thick. Cut into 1" (2.5 cm) strips and lay 1 strip on top of another then press together in the centre with the back of a knife. Pull into long strips and slip into the wok of boiling oil. Deep fry over moderate heat. Press and turn occasionally until the doughnut is inflated and brown. Remove and drain.*

GENERAL TERMS IN DIM SUM

1. BAKE :
To cook in the oven with dry heat.

2. BAKE BLIND :
Line a pie shell with grease proof paper and half-fill with raw rice or beans. Bake in a hot oven till the pastry is nearly cooked. Remove the rice or beans and paper then return the pastry shell to the oven to complete baking.

3. BIND :
To add liquid or egg to a mixture in order to hold it together.

4. BLEND :
To mix ingredients together to form a smooth paste.

5. BRUSH :
To put beaten egg or thin syrup on the surface of the pastry to give a glossy appearance.

6. CHOP :
To cut roughly into tiny pieces.

7. COAT :
To cover or to brush food with flour, egg, crumbs or batter.

8. CREAM :
To mix ingredients, often fat and sugar, to the consistency of cream.

9. DRAW IN :
To fold flour into the ingredients to mix together.

10. DECORATE :
To furnish with ornamental ingredients.

11. DICE :
To cut into even cubes.

12. **FOLD :**

To blend ingredients together gently and slowly.

13. **KNEAD :**

To pull and stretch the dough in order to develop the gluten strength and so to ensure an even texture and volume.

14. **PINCH :**

To draw the edges of the pastry together to seal tightly.

15. **POUND ·**

To beat against the table or in a large bowl in order to make the texture of the ingredient(s) elastic and firm.

16. **PROVE :**

To allow the dough to rise.

17. **RUB IN :**

To mix the fat and flour together by using only the finger tips to work on the ingredients.

18. **SCALD :**

To heat milk almost to boiling point.

19. **SIFT :**

To shake dry ingredients through a sieve to remove lumps.

20. **STIR :**

To move ingredients in circles to mix evenly.

21. **WHISK :**

To beat briskly, for thickening cream or egg.

22. **WORK IN :**

To fold flour into the centre to mix with other ingredients.

23. **WRAP :**

To fold up pastry to enclose the filling.

辨五穀 · 釋疑難

五穀之中，米及玉蜀黍多生於熱帶地區，爲東方人之主要食糧。小麥、大麥及粿麥則產於溫帶，爲西方人所重用，以下是五穀之分析及用途介紹：

1 米： 以米作食糧之人口幾佔地球之半，產於中國、印度、日本、暹羅等地，用途廣闊，種類亦多，主要分爲二大類：

    A 粘米——燒飯、煮粥、釀酒等。

    粘米粉——蒸糕、煎咸薄餅、製造發粉。

    炒米粉——軟、硬炒米餅。

    B 糯米——包粽、有味飯、甜粥等。

    糯米粉——年糕、湯團、軟糍。

    熟糯粉（即糕粉）——餅餡、香蕉糕。

2 小麥： 以小麥作食糧之人口亦佔地球之半，最普遍用途爲製造麵包、麵條。主要分二大類：

    A 硬麥——多產於乾燥陽光充足之地如加拿大。含大量蛋白質，使人精力充沛。麥粒堅硬，蛋白質含量約十至十五％。韌性強、含有大量麵筋原料——麩素。磨粉後即爲筋粉。粉中之筋與水混和後轉韌，使麵團有彈性。放焗爐加熱後則膨脹，以致成爲鬆軟之麵飽。

    1 高筋粉——蛋白含量爲十二至十五％。宜做通心粉、意粉、油條、麵包、擘酥等。

    2 中筋粉——蛋白含量約十至十二％。宜做酥餅雲吞皮之類。

    3 汀麵——將筋粉放於布袋中，置水盆內揉之。揉出之粉質沉於水中，晒乾後即爲汀麵。宜做蝦餃粉果等。袋中黏性麵團則爲麵筋。

    B 軟麥——產於較陰暗潮濕地區如西歐、英國、美國東部等地。麵粒剖開後呈粉狀。蛋白含量約七至十％，韌性較弱，磨粉後即成普通麵粉。

    1 普通麵粉——餅乾、乾果蛋糕、批皮、曲奇、克力架、冬栗等。（糕餅甜品書中將有詳述。）

    2 自發粉——普通麵粉一磅加梳打粉 $\frac{1}{4}$ 安加他他粉 $\frac{3}{8}$ 安混合篩勻即可。宜做簡便蛋糕、脆漿等。

3 大麥： 最能適應環境，能生長於貧瘠之土壤中。

    A 整粒——多用於製麥芽以供：

    1 釀酒

    2 製麥芽糖

    B 加工後成爲洋薏米——宜煮湯及作紅燒肉之配料，與檸檬混和製成菓汁。

4 粿麥：以為一種既黑且硬之穀粒，味帶酸。產於較冷地帶及劣
　　　　土中。鈣質比其他穀類較高，為歐陸中層社會人仕之主
　　　　要食糧，粿麥粉之麵筋含量極少，故難獨當一面製造麵
　　　　包，多與小麥粉同用。
　　　　Ａ粿麥粉——製造黑麵包及一種薄餅乾。
　　　　Ｂ製造威士忌、毡酒、伏特加等。

5 玉蜀黍：（又名粟米）產於較熱地方如美國、意大利等國家之
　　　　南部。
　　　　Ａ整個放於水中、加糖焗熟，塗牛油而食。
　　　　Ｂ將粟米粒削出，與其他什菜粒肉丁混合炒熟做菜。
　　　　Ｃ粟米可搾油及製粟膠。
　　　　Ｄ粟米粉及吉士粉——做布甸、糕餅、有凝結作用。
　　　　Ｅ漿粉——漿硬衣服、床單等、並可製漿糊。

點心常用術語解釋

1. **烘**——不用油而放入焗爐中焗至乾硬。
2. **塗油**——搽上油或流質於食物上使其不致乾燥，尤其適用於
　　　　炙肉時。
3. **混合**——將固體或流質之材料混在一起。
4. **塗蛋**——將打勻之蛋黃液體塗在批皮上使其光澤。
5. **切碎**——將食物剁成小塊。
6. **裹**——把食物滾上一層麵粉、麵包糠、粉漿或蛋液。
7. **打軟**——將材料混合（多數以油、糖為主）搞拌成奶油狀。
8. **製飾**——將蛋糕或餅加彩色裝飾物點綴之。
9. **切細**——切成均等骰子狀。
10. **覆入**——慢慢捲入拌勻。
11. **搓**——反覆按勻粉糰，令粉中麵筋發揮作用，和成一塊軟
　　　　滑粉糰。
12. **捏**——將粉糰邊沿向入捏成花紋。
13. **發**——使粉糰發起。
14. **擦入**——將硬牛油放入麵粉中擦成碎屑。
15. **篩**——除去塊狀麵粉及雜質。
16. **蒸**——放於蒸籠內隔水用猛火蒸燉。
17. **攪拌**——以順時鐘或反時鐘方向搞動和勻。
18. **打起**——以快速手法打蛋白或忌廉使其濃厚。
19. **撥**——將麵粉撥入中央。
20. **包起**——以窩形盛載餡料，然後封口。

CEREALS AND FLOUR

While rice and maize are grown in tropical regions and are widely eaten in Asia, wheat, barley and rye are grown in temperate regions and are more important in the daily diet of Europeans. The following explains what the different types of cereals and flour are:

1. *Rice is the major food for Asian people. Rice is grown in China, India, Japan, Thailand and Burma. There are many different kinds of rice which can be used in various ways but in general, rice is divided into two main streams:*

   a. *Whole grain plain rice is used in steamed plain rice, congee and fermented rice wine. Rice flour is used to make puddings, cakes and baking powder. Cooked rice flour can be used to make hard and soft cakes.*

   b. *Whole grain glutinous rice is used to make dumplings, flavoured rice and sweet soup. When ground into a powder form, glutinous rice flour can be used to make Chinese New Year pudding, rice balls and soft cakes. Cooked glutinous rice flour can be used in cake filling and to make other Chinese sweets.*

2. *Wheat is widely used by half of the world's population to make bread and noodles. Wheat is also divided into two main streams:*

   a. *Hard wheat is grown in the driest and sunny areas of Canada. It contains 10% to 15% protein which gives us strength. The wheat grain appears strong and flinty when dissected. When it is ground into a powder form, it is called 'high protein flour' or 'bread flour'. Mix the flour with water and an elastic dough will be formed. This elastic dough can then be used to make bread.*

      i. *High protein flour contains 12% to 15% protein and is used to make macaroni, bread, crisps and deep fried crullers.*

      ii. *Low protein flour contains 10% to 12% protein and is used to make crisps and won ton pastry.*

      iii. *Wheat starch can be made by kneading some protein flour with water & placing the mixture into a cotton bag in a basin of water. This is then kneaded further until the powder inside filters out. When the remaining water evaporates, the sediment is the wheat starch. Wheat starch is used to make dumplings and raviolies. The sticky flour dough left inside the bag is "gluten".*

b. Soft wheat is grown in dull and wet climates such as western Europe and the Eastern United States of America. The grain has a floury cross section and contains 7% to 10% protein.

    i. Soft wheat can be ground into a powder called plain flour. Plain flour dough is not springy and is used to make biscuits, short crust pastry, cookies, crackers and fruit cakes.

    ii. Self raising flour can be made by mixing 1 lb (½ kg) plain flour with ¼ oz (7 g) bicarbonate soda and ⅜ oz (10½ g) cream of tartar. It is used for baking plain cakes and for making batter.

3. Barley can be grown in poor soil.

    a. Barley grains are usually used to make beer or malt.

    b. Barley kernels are made into pearl barley, which is usually used to make soups and puddings. The pearl barley must be stripped of its sheath and polished before use. Nutritious barley drinks can also be made from boiling pearl barley.

4. Rye is a kind of dark and hard cereal which is grown in cold climates. Rye contains more calcium than any other cereals and has a sour taste. Rye is widely used in Europe. Rye flour contains little gluten, which holds the bread together, so it should be used together with wheat flour. Rye can also be used to make whisky, gin and vodka.

5. Maize is grown in tropical regions such as South America and Southern Italy. Maize can be boiled and eaten on the cob. The whole maize kernels can be removed from the cob and used with other ingredients. The cooked maize kernels can also be ground into a cream to make soup. Maize can be used to make cooking oil and also syrups for cakes. When it is ground into a powder form, the starch (corn starch) can be used to make cakes, pudding or gravy. It can also be used to straighten cloth and materials or used as glue.

Our Cooking Centre

Chinese Cookery Courses

Chinese Dishes Course
Chinese Roasts Course
Dim Sum Course
Cakes & Pastries Course
Professional Bread-making Course
Bean Curd Course
Moon Cake Course
Piping Course
Wedding Cake Course
Ingredients Course
Banquet Dishes Course
Vegetable Carving Course
Deep Fried Pastry Course

* * * * * * *

½-3 days Tourist Group Course
1 day Selected Course
1-week Tourist Course
4-week Intensive Course
8-week Intensive Course
13-week Professional Course
17-week Teacher Training Course

Length of course:—
     2 hours to 17 weeks

Our Hostel

* Air-conditioning
* Colour T.V.
* Private bath
* Private telephone
* Reasonable rent

3-DAY TOURIST GROUP COURSE

US$300.00 per head for a group of 10 to 15 persons
Schedule as follows—

Time	Day 1	Day 2	Day 3
10 am	2 Chinese dishes	2 Chinese dishes	Market Visit
12 noon	A taste of Chinese dishes	A taste of dim sum	2 dish sum
2 pm	2 dim sum	2 Chinese dishes	2 dim sum
4 pm	Chinese dish practice	Chinese dish practice	Chinese dish practice

Prices valid within 1 year.

120

嘉饌家政中心暫時尚未在任何國家開設分校。

各式烹飪班

各省中菜班
初高燒烤班
初高點心班
高級西餅班
職業麵包班
馳名豆腐班
速成月餅班
速成唧花班
結婚禮餅班
各式原料班
筵席大菜班
蔬菓雕花班
各式油器班
1/2—3天集體遊客班
1天各科精選班
1週遊客班
4週速成班
8週速成班
13週職業班
17週教師訓練班

宿舍設備

＊空氣調節
＊彩色電視
＊私家浴室
＊私人電話
＊合理價錢

"CHOPSTICKS RECIPES"

is a symbol of   CONFIDENCE

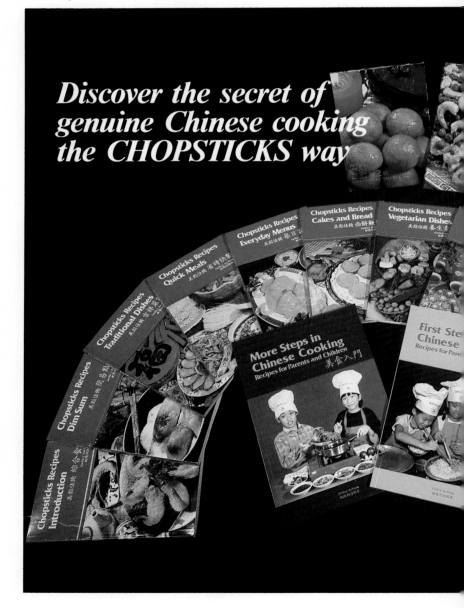

Discover the secret of genuine Chinese cooking the CHOPSTICKS way

Chopsticks Recipes Everyday Menus 美點佳餚 每日
Chopsticks Recipes Cakes and Bread 美點佳餚 西餅麵
Chopsticks Recipes Vegetarian Dishes 美點佳餚 養生素
Chopsticks Recipes Quick Meals 美點佳餚 省時快餐
Chopsticks Recipes Traditional Dishes 美點佳餚 古法
Chopsticks Recipes Dim Sum 美點佳餚 包餃點
Chopsticks Recipes Introduction 美點佳餚 綜合食

More Steps in Chinese Cooking
Recipes for Parents and Children 美食入門

First Ste
Chinese
Recipes for Pare

CHOPSTICKS PUBLICATIONS
a symbol of confidence

The **Chopsticks Recipes** series English-Chinese bilingual edition (128 pp 105 gsm matt art paper) is an encyclopedia to Chinese cuisine, written for people who enjoy trying different kinds of Chinese food in their daily life. Book 1 is an introduction to a variety of cooking while each of the other 11 books contain one specific subject.

Book 1 — **introduction**
Book 2 — **Dim Sum**
Book 3 — **Traditional Dishes**
Book 4 — **Quick Meals**
Book 5 — **Everyday Menus**
Book 6 — **Cakes and Bread**
Book 7 — **Vegetarian Dishes**
Book 8 — **More Dim Sum**
Book 9 — **Budget Meals**
Book 10 — **Chinese Casseroles**
Book 11 — **Healthy Bean Dishes**
Book 12 — **Vegetable Carvings**

First Steps in Chinese Cooking and **More Steps in Chinese Cooking** English-Chinese bilingual edition (96 pp 115 gsm matt art paper) each contains 42 specially written recipes which have been tested by children from the ages of 8 to 14 years. These book are designed for parents and children to learn Chinese cooking together.

Other Chopsticks publications include **Chopsticks Cookery Cards** Grades 1 and 2 English-Chinese bilingual edition (260 gsm B/S coated art board with pp lamination)

Chopsticks Recipes revised English Edition (128 pp 128 gsm matt art paper)

Chopsticks Wok Miracles English-Chinese bilingual edition (128 pp 128 gsm matt art paper)

包餅用具

Baking Utensils

包餅用具

(1)車輪包模   (9)搽盞
(2)磅   (10)忌廉筒
(3)蛋拂   (11)紙包蛋糕模
(4)方包模   (12)蛋搽盞
(5)雞批盞   (13)括刀
(6)餅鏟   (14)量杯
(7)花級   (15)套裝花級
(8)量匙   (16)粉篩

Baking Utensils

① Golden Wheel Mould
② Scale
③ Egg Beater
④ White Bread Mould
⑤ Chicken Pie Shells
⑥ Cake Server
⑦ Cutters
⑧ Measuring Spoons
⑨ Tart Shells
⑩ Cream Horn Moulds
⑪ Portuguese Sponge Moulds
⑫ Egg Tart Shells
⑬ Scraping Knife
⑭ Measuring Cups
⑮ Cutter-set
⑯ Sieve

Hand-made Wooden Moulds

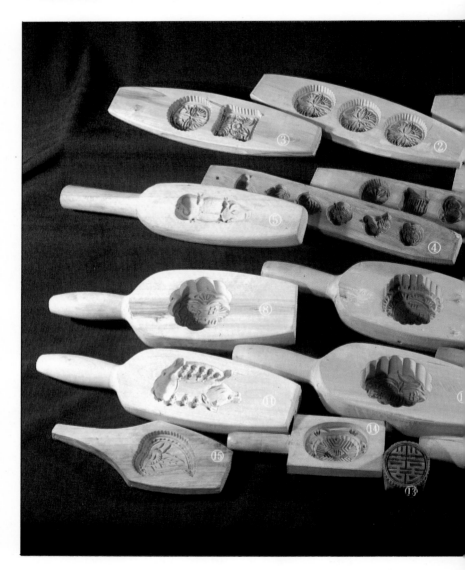

各款木雕餅模

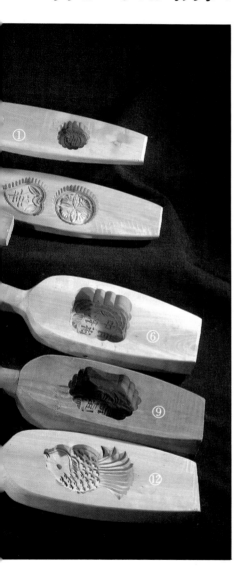

各款木雕餅模

(1)棋子餅模
(2)三眼水晶餅模
(3)雙眼水晶餅模
(4)六眼水晶餅模
(5)豬仔餅模
(6)方型月餅模
(7)海棠型月餅模
(8)圓型月餅模
(9)六角型月餅模
(10)橢圓型月餅模
(11)豬婆模
(12)金魚模
(13)雙囍印
(14)龜模
(15)桃模

Hand-made Wooden Moulds

① Mini Cake Mould
② Crystal Cake A
③ Crystal Cake B
④ Crystal Cake C
⑤ Piggy Mould
⑥ Moon Cake Mould A
⑦ Moon Cake Mould B
⑧ Moon Cake Mould C
⑨ Moon Cake Mould D
⑩ Moon Cake Mould E
⑪ Mother Pig Mould
⑫ Fish Mould
⑬ Double-happiness Stamp
⑭ Tortoise Mould
⑮ Peach Mould

OVEN TEMPERATURE

Description of Oven	Approx. Temperature (Centre of Oven)		Gas Mark		
	(^{O}F)	(^{O}C)		(^{O}F)	(^{O}C)
Very low	200-250	100-130	¼ =225	107	
			½ =250	130	
Cool	250-300	130-150	1 =275	140	
			2 =300	150	
Warm to moderate	300-350	150-180	3 =325	170	
			4 =350	180	
Moderate	350-375	180-190	5 =375	190	
			6 =400	200	
Fairly hot	375-400	190-210	7 =425	220	
			8 =450	230	
Hot to very hot	425-450	220-225	9 =475	240	
			10=500	250	
Very hot	450-500	230-250	10=500	250	

LIQUID MEASURES

(approximate equivalence)

¼	pint	=	½	cup	=	4 fluid oz	=	125ml
½	pint	=	1	cup	=	8 fluid oz	=	250ml
¾	pint	=	1½	cups	=	12 fluid oz	=	375ml
1	pint	=	2	cups	=	16 fluid oz	=	500ml
1½	pints	=	3	cups	=	24 fluid oz	=	750ml
2	pints (1 quart)	=	4	cups	=	32 fluid oz	=	1000ml